ROY OLIVER

THE WANDERER
AND THE WAY

ROY OLIVER

THE WANDERER
AND THE WAY

THE HEBREW TRADITION
IN THE WRITINGS OF
MARTIN BUBER

EAST AND WEST LIBRARY

MADE IN GREAT BRITAIN
PRINTED BY WESTERN PRINTING SERVICES LTD · BRISTOL

דָּרַשְׁתִּי קִרְבָתְךָ בְּכָל־לִבִּי קְרָאתִיךָ
יָצָאתִי לִקְרָאתְךָ לִקְרָאתִי מְצָאתִיךָ

Longing I sought Thy presence;
LORD, with my whole heart did I call and pray,
And going out toward Thee,
I found Thee coming to me on the way.

From *God in All* by Jehudah Halevi,
rhymed translation by Nina Salaman

for my son

ADRIAN DAVID

CONTENTS

Foreword   ix

Introduction   1

1. The Wanderer: Adam   20

2. The Wandering People: Noah   39

3. The Wayfarer: Abraham   57

4. The Wayfaring People: Moses   78

5. The End of the Way of Man: Psalmist   95

6. The Way of the World: Isaiah   116

7. The Way: The Servant   135

Book List   153

Notes and References   161

FOREWORD

AFTER some years of study of the works of Martin Buber the writing of this book was begun in the spring of 1965. The full draft had progressed as far as the end of chapter five by Pentecost, concluding with Buber's views on death and redemption and the lines from his favourite Psalm, 73. The news from Jerusalem was that he had been discharged from hospital and was making a good recovery from the fall in which he fractured a hip. In the following week the writer re-read *The Prophetic Faith* once more but for some reason not a line of the sixth chapter could be drafted. Then the Press reported that after the next Jewish Sabbath Buber did not live to see the sun set again. It is strange. The writer felt like someone in a Pirandello play. He had known Buber almost exclusively from English versions of his books. The books were still there and the voice that spoke from them was as clear and strong as ever. This is one reason why, in the final revision, it was decided not to change everything from present tense to past.

This book about Mordecai Martin Buber is written by someone with no special qualifications, from a sense of personal indebtedness to Buber for his teaching which he no doubt shares with many people, famous and unknown, in many parts of the world; and partly because there had been no book about Buber written by an Englishman. It is not a critique but an appreciation. It is not a full account of Buber's 'thought' but an attempt to show that it is his lifelong response to the Hebrew Bible that enables us to see his Hasidic writings and his I–Thou 'philosophy' —in all its varied applications—in their true dimensions. In other words, it tries to illustrate the hardly novel but often conveniently forgotten truth that Buber was as much a Jew as his full name implies.

The initial problem was, how to find a non-conceptual pattern which would evoke Buber as a human person. The last and obvious place where an answer was sought seems the right one. It is hoped that the Biblical archetypes—Adam, Noah, Abraham, Moses, Psalmist, Isaiah and Servant—will throw light on Buber as a man and not merely as an oracular source of doctrines

ix

or ideas. Each chapter moves from Buber's response to the
Biblical human figure which is its subject, through the Hasidic
material in which Buber traces the same theme, and finally to its
expression in the contemporary formulation usually referred to
as his I and Thou 'philosophy'.

No apology is offered for the great amount of direct quotation
in this book. It is a sound Jewish tradition that teaching, which
comes from a whole man, should be passed on in the teacher's
own words wherever possible. This is particularly true of one who
used words as Buber did. It is hoped that the constant quotations
will remind the reader that it is to Buber's own books that his
attention is invited. The interwoven commentary is there to con-
nect the quotations and give some incidental justification of the
selection made.

Buber began one address in this way:

> We are living in an age of the depreciation of words. The
> intellect with its gift for language has been all too willing
> to put itself at the disposal of whatever trends prevail at the
> time. Instead of letting the words grow out of the thought in
> responsible silence, the intellect has manufactured words for
> every demand with almost mechanical skill. It is not only
> the intellectuals, who are now finding a suspicious reception
> for their disquisitions, who must suffer for this 'treason'.
> What is worse is that their audience, above all the entire
> younger generation of our time, is deprived of the noblest
> happiness of youth: the happiness of believing in the
> spirit . . .[1]

He 'entered into the word'[2] he spoke with a responsibility easily
missed by the casual or sceptical reader. In the Ethics of the
Fathers (from the Mishnah, quoted in the Jewish Prayer Book)
we read that the Torah is acquired by forty-eight qualifications.
The first is 'by audible study'. Buber recommends it for study of
the Hebrew Bible. It may also be recommended to readers of
Buber, who will thereby make a more than merely mental effort
to receive what is more than an intellectual or verbal formulation. Anyone who had the good fortune to hear him speak will

---

[1] IW. 234. For book-list and abbreviations used in references (which are
at the end of the book) see p. 153.
[2] TR. 29.

not think it eccentric or excessive to treat Buber's printed words in that way. Which is not to say that Buber's words are of Biblical authority.

The reader need not brace himself for any strenuous feats of metaphysic and dialectic. At an early stage of study, determined to come up with something impressive, the writer thought he might have found a source of Buber's famous terminology[1] in the *Zohar* and wrote to him at some length about it. The reply, from a Lucerne sanatorium, was in one sentence:

> The term 'I and Thou' in my book is the result not of reading but of personal experience only.

It should be added that it looks—it is not quite certain—as though Buber had put the full stop after 'experience' and then, setting aside all he had derived from reading, added the emphatic 'only'. He offers not his thought but his whole life of encounter.

What the writer shares with his publishers and helpers— among whom must be gratefully mentioned several members of the Faculty of the Hebrew University in Jerusalem—is the conviction that Buber's views should be presented without soft-pedalling or apology. They are not completely digestible by orthodox Jews or orthodox Christians and they may make the modern reader who is a dogmatic secularist uncomfortable at times. For this reason the writer wishes to say, though he was not asked to do so, that he is solely responsible for what appears here. This applies particularly to Dr. Malcolm L. Diamond of Princeton University (to whose own excellent book on Buber reference will be made), Rabbi Louis Jacobs, Ph.D., and Rabbi Isaac Newman, who kindly read the full draft and thereby ensured

---

[1] In 'The History of the Dialogical Principle', printed as the Afterword to the 1965 edition of *Between Man and Man*, Buber wrote: 'In all ages it has undoubtedly been glimpsed that the reciprocal essential relationship between two beings signifies a primal opportunity of being, and one, in fact, that enters into the phenomenon that man exists. And it has also ever again been glimpsed that just through the fact that he enters into essential reciprocity, man becomes revealed as man; indeed, that only with this and through this does he attain to that valid participation in being that is reserved for him; thus, that the saying of Thou by the I stands in the origin of all individual becoming.' Buber then goes on to trace the usage of the phrase 'I and Thou' from a letter written in 1775 by F. H. Jacobi to an unknown person (quoted in a letter of 1781 from Jacobi to Lavater).

that the book is not inaccurate or misleading in its references to traditional Judaism. At a later stage the book was read by Martin Buber's old friend Professor S. H. Bergman of the Hebrew University and by his best-known interpreter, Professor Maurice S. Friedman, to both of whom the writer is grateful.

The author and publishers are also grateful to the following publishers and translators for permission to quote from English versions of works by Martin Buber and from other authors quoted in this work:

GEORGE ALLEN & UNWIN LTD.: *The Knowledge of Man*, translated by Maurice Friedman; T. & T. CLARK (and CHARLES SCRIBNER'S SONS): *I and Thou*, translated by Ronald Gregor Smith; COMMENTARY (New York): *Speeches on Judaism*, translated by Ralph Manheim (American Jewish Committee); EAST AND WEST LIBRARY: *Moses, Israel and Palestine*, translated by Stanley Godman, and *The Legend of the Baal-Shem*, translated by Maurice Friedman; HARPER & ROW: *The Prophetic Faith*, translated by Norman P. Goldhawk, *Hasidism and Modern Man*, translated by Maurice Friedman, and *Eclipse of God*, translated by Maurice Friedman, Eugene Kamenka, Norbert Guterman and I. M. Lask; HORIZON PRESS: *The Tales of Rabbi Nachman*, translated by Maurice Friedman; THE JEWISH PUBLICATION SOCIETY OF AMERICA: *For the Sake of Heaven*, translated by Ludwig Lewisohn, and *Studies in Judaism* (Schecter); JUDAISM (New York): 'Abraham the Seer', translated by Sophie Meyer; THE MACMILLAN COMPANY: *Paths in Utopia*, translated by R. F. C. Hull; ROUTLEDGE & KEGAN PAUL: *Between Man and Man*, translated by Ronald Gregor Smith, *Images of Good and Evil*, translated by Michael Bullock, and *Pointing the Way*, translated by Maurice Friedman; SCHOCKEN BOOKS: *Israel and the World*, translated by Greta Hort, Olga Marx, I. M. Lask and Maurice Friedman, *Tales of the Hasidim* (I Early Masters, II Later Masters), translated by Olga Marx, *Ten Rungs*, translated by Olga Marx, *Addresses on Judaism* (*At the Turning*, etc.) and (both by N. N. Glatzer) *On Jewish Learning*, and *Franz Rosenzweig—His Life and Thought*; CHARLES SCRIBNER'S SONS: *Good and Evil* (*Images of Good and Evil* and *Right and Wrong*), translated by Michael Bullock and Ronald Gregor Smith; MARTIN SECKER & WARBURG: *The Last of the Just* (Schwarz-Bart), translated by Stephen Becker; STUDENT CHRISTIAN MOVEMENT PRESS: *Right and Wrong*, translated by Ronald Gregor Smith; A. P. WATT & SON: *The Outline of History* (Wells). A few other brief quotations are acknowledged in the text and notes. Part of Chapter 5 first appeared in the December 1966 issue of THE ARYAN PATH (Bombay).

ROY OLIVER

Ipswich, Suffolk
December 1966

THE WANDERER AND THE WAY

INTRODUCTION

ALL subsequent writers on Martin Buber are indebted to his faithful translator and interpreter, Professor Maurice S. Friedman. From the bibliography in Friedman's standard work, *Martin Buber: The Life of Dialogue*, there emerges a somewhat curious picture of Buber's first appearance in print in the English-speaking world. Until after the Second World War, almost[1] the only book of Buber's to be published in England was the translation of the most important single work of his European period, *I and Thou*,[2] by the Rev. Ronald Gregor Smith. This was in 1937, fifteen years after the appearance of *Ich und Du* in Germany. *I and Thou* is indeed a landmark in Buber's lifework as well as in the religious literature of our time. It is right that it is by this book that he should have become known in the English-speaking world. A young Christian minister told the writer that his Cambridge tutor had read it no less than five hundred times.

But the continued concentration on *I and Thou*, to the virtual exclusion of Buber's later work, is also perhaps partly due to the fact that it was, until 1945, the only book of Buber's widely known in English. This has given rise to a widespread misconception, strengthened no doubt by Buber's growing influence which extends, as Will Herberg puts it, not only in the fields of theology and philosophy but among scholars, educators, writers, poets, artists, sociologists, physicians, psychotherapists and social workers. 'It has often been suggested to me', Buber has written,[3] with a courteous irony that needs no additional emphasis, 'that I should liberate this teaching from its "confessional limitations", as people like to put it, and proclaim it as an unfettered teaching of mankind. Taking such a "universal" path would have been for me pure arbitrariness. In order to speak to the world what I have heard, I am not bound to step into the street. I may remain standing in the door of my ancestral home: here too the word that it uttered does not go astray.' Talk of Buber's 'philosophy', even of his 'religious existentialism', wanders from the vital truth. For Martin Buber his teaching is dynamic Judaism, as he understands and has endeavoured to live it, or it is nothing.

After the Second World War, the publishing situation changed radically. More than a score of Buber's works have appeared since 1945 in England and the United States (where a dozen have already passed into still wider circulation in paperback editions), virtually the full range of his post-European work is now available and some early works are beginning to appear too. The first post-war publication in America seems to have been the unique Hasidic chronicle, *For the Sake of Heaven* (*Gog and Magog*) in 1945. Two other works appeared in England in the following year. One—now almost entirely superseded by later collections —also contained some of Buber's writings on Hasidism.[4] The other was one his major works of Biblical interpretation, *Moses*. Since then the tide of important works, all written after their author was sixty, has continued to flow. But nearly all these books fall, as to subject-matter anyway, into the three categories indicated by those works already named. They belong to the formulation in contemporary terms which is usually referred to as the I and Thou 'philosophy'; to the renovation and explication of the eighteenth-century revival in Eastern European Jewry known as Hasidism, which Buber virtually saved from obloquy and oblivion; or they deal directly with the Hebrew Bible.

But classification by subject-matter does not tell the whole truth. As most writers on Buber have well understood, the three elements interpenetrate, the three 'levels' are all there in every book, though in one book or another one or other of them occupies the foreground. In one way, therefore, it matters little whether an account of Buber's work begins with the I and Thou 'philosophy'—which is more likely to attract contemporary intellectuals than an approach through an unfamiliar eighteenth-century Jewish folk movement in Eastern Europe that almost seems to move counter to the tides of modern history—or with what might be received as merely one more piece of Biblical exegesis—or with Hasidism, which will appeal to aesthetes because of the beautiful legendary 'literature' that Buber has restored and its intriguing pictures of a colourful religious life in small communities; even Allen Ginsberg and Norman Mailer respond to this. Of course all responsible writers trace Buber's teaching to the taproot of the Hebrew Bible but this remains, on the whole, the least stressed of the three elements. That may be explained in terms of the *zeitgeist* of a Christian and now largely post-Christian Western civilization. But there seems to be room and occasion for one more book on the teaching of Martin Buber in which he is seen, as he himself puts it, 'standing in the door of my ancestral home'. To the strictly traditional Jew it may seem that he has opened that door dangerously wide on an uncomprehending and partly hostile world and is leaning from it so perilously that he might himself fall. [5] The present writer, who is not able to stand formally as a Christian or as a Jew, sees him otherwise, as custodian and also as patient host. At times, indeed, he seems to see not so much a patriarchal figure in one of the portals of an ancient Temple as a great light that blazes out around it into the surrounding gloom. Buber points beyond himself.

* * *

There are two basic ways in which the interpreter of the lifework of a great man may proceed. The temporal one, in which he tries to trace the chronological development of a long lifetime. And the spatial one, in which he contemplates the whole group of works and tries to apprehend the pattern as a whole, though it is one that changes even while it remains the same, as one approaches in different moods and at different times. With Martin Buber, the first method would lead from his earlier concern with Occidental and Oriental mysticism to Hasidism (though he was first introduced to and impressed by Hasidism as a child). From thence to the maturity of *I and Thou*, published when its author was forty-five, in which apprehensions of spiritual union finally fade before the vision of the eternal dialogue. And so on to the works of Biblical interpretation, mostly written after he had come to Jerusalem at the age of sixty. The spatial approach, which is mainly followed in this book—though the movement of each chapter from the Biblical through the Hasidic to the modern follows the wider chronology of historic manifestation—sees the pattern otherwise and gives to Buber's work as faithful translator and interpreter of the Hebrew Bible a centrality that is almost entirely lacking in some other assessments of Buber's life work. The spatial approach has also been preferred because it diverges as far as possible from systematic intellectual analysis and offers the writer some of the opportunities of the portrait painter. Just as Martin Buber prefaces *I and Thou* with an epigraph from

Goethe which speaks of 'God's presence in each element', so he believes that we meet as much as we are permitted to know of the mystery of a great writer or speaker through what we make of what we find in each and all of his works:

> When we really understand a poem, all we know of the poet is what we learn of him in the poem—no biographical wisdom is of value for the pure understanding of what is to be understood: the *I* which approaches us is the subject of this single poem. But when we read other poems by the poet in the same true way their subjects combine in all their multiplicity, completing and confirming one another, to form the one polyphony of the person's existence.[6]

Indeed, we may almost say that in Buber we meet nothing else. "I, myself, have no 'doctrine' ", he wrote at the end of the Foreword to the 1953 edition of *For the Sake of Heaven*:

> My function is to point out realities of this order. He who expects of me a teaching other than a pointing out of this character, will always be disillusioned. And it would seem to me, indeed, that in this hour of history the crucial thing is not to possess a fixed doctrine, but rather to recognize eternal reality and out of its depth to be able to face the reality of the present. No way can be pointed to in this desert night. One's purpose must be to help men of today to stand fast, with their soul in readiness, until the dawn breaks and a path becomes visible where none suspected it.

He hopes, he wrote elsewhere,[7] for two kinds of readers: for those who know about the reality to which he points a finger and those who deny this reality. 'The mere *inimicus*, as which I regard everyone who wishes to relegate me to the realm of ideology and there let my thoughts count, I would gladly dispense with.' It was also Goethe who said of a German writer that 'we learn nothing by reading him, but we *become* something'.[8] We become, each according to his capacity and his unique way, what man should become in relationship to man, and through the only mediation by which true relationship can be approached: the Word, spoken or unspoken.

But it is also true that, as Buber says of some great Hasidic utterances, the words spontaneously spoken can best be understood in the light of the situation and event to which they were the response of a whole heart. In this introduction, therefore, we may well follow in outline the chronology of the man's life as it stands in high relief against the dark background of European and Palestinian history in our time. Buber has himself referred to 'the massacre of millions of Jews' and 'the establishment of a Jewish State' as 'astounding phenomena of living and dying' that 'have at last brought before the world the fact of the existence of Jewry as a fact of particular significance, and from this point Judaism itself begins to be seen'.[9] His own migration from the catastrophe of assimilationism to the new ingathering of Israel already in his lifetime seemed to bear about it something of the aura of authentic myth.

* * *

We have mentioned that *I and Thou* was the only work of Buber's widely known in the English-speaking world before the Second World War and that it first appeared in Germany as early as 1923. It was also almost the only major work that Buber wrote between that date and 1938 when he left Europe. True, he was serving as Professor of Jewish Religion and Ethics—it later became, History of Religions—at the University of Frankfurt am Main from 1923 until the Nazis came to power. (Franz Rosenzweig, for whom the appointment was intended, nominated Buber when his illness made it impossible for him to accept; and it was said that Paul Tillich also used his good offices on Buber's behalf.) But something more is necessary to explain the diminution of the flow of major works from so prolific a writer and it is not far to seek.

Perhaps because Buber's full stature had begun to be realized after the publication of *Ich und Du*, he was approached in the spring of 1925 by a young Christian publisher in Berlin, Lambert Schneider, to undertake a new translation into German of the Hebrew Bible. This must have been the supreme challenge to Martin Buber as a deeply religious Jew. Before the First World War he had dreamed of such a translation, to be made by collective Jewish effort. Now the call had come to him and not only from a publisher. In *Confession of the Writer*, a poem Buber wrote for Ernst Simon in 1945 (given here in Maurice Friedman's translation, from his forthcoming edition of Buber's *Gleanings: A Believing Humanism,* where it will be accompanied by the German text and a note on the word-play) he looks back to the early days of his work on the Hasidic legends and evokes the transformation that came upon him when he felt summoned to render the Hebrew Scripture:

> Once with a light keel
> I shipped out to the land of legends
> Through the storm of deeds and play,
> With my gaze fixed on the goal
> And in my blood the beguiling poison—
> Then one descended to me
> Who seized me by the hair
> And spoke: Now render the Scriptures!
>
> From that hour on the galley
> Keeps my brain and hands on course,
> The rudder writes characters,
> My life disdains its honor
> And the soul forgets that it sang.
> All storms must stand and bow
> When cruelling compelling in the silence
> The speech of the spirit resounds.
>
> Hammer your deeds in the rock, world!
> The Word is wrought in the flood.

Yet the author of *I and Thou* would not accept the publisher's commission single-handed. He agreed only on a condition that, if pondered, reveals something of his understanding of what the Hebrew Bible teaches about the relationship between man and man and what it is that binds them together. Buber stipulated that the work must be borne jointly by himself and Franz Rosenzweig. That Rosenzweig was one of the most gifted European Jews of this century is proven by his famous book *The Star of Redemption,* largely written on postcards sent home from the trenches. But now composition could only be far more fragmentary even than that. In 1921 Rosenzweig had been attacked by an illness that was expected to end his life within a year. In the following year he was able to lecture from his bed, but by the end of it he could no longer write or speak distinctly, he was becoming completely paralysed. From spring 1923 onwards he could communicate only with a special typewriter which would print a single letter after each turn of a dial. Buber would undertake to translate the Hebrew Bible only with this man. His own work was multiplied by having to prepare everything in detail for his afflicted friend. It may be supposed that he thus helped to prolong and enrich Rosenzweig's life until nearly the end of 1929, five years in which the friends produced between them ten books of the Bible. Afterwards Buber went on alone and completed five more Books (reckoning the twelve 'minor' prophets as one) before the rise of Nazism challenged him to find the deed that expressed the Word. This surely is why there were so few works by Buber himself in the years 1925–1938? He had virtually dedicated his life to the Hebrew Bible and to bringing its message to his oppressed Jewish countrymen. No man could foresee that his greatest output would follow after the age of sixty.

In a booklet accompanying the translation of the *Psalms*, Buber declared that the Hebrew Bible is a single whole consisting of linguistically inter-related parts that explain and illuminate one another, it is a single theological unit, a 'Theologumenon'. He had striven to convey the peculiar rhythm of the spoken word, still audible to him in the original text, by way of 'kolometrie', in which the unit of breath corresponds to the unit of meaning. So determined was he to render every remaining trace of the oral tradition that he endeavoured to retain repetitions of words and word-stems. Frequently he resorted to transliteration, regardless of whether the words thus coined did or did not already exist in the German language. The first appearance of a word and its relationship to the immediate context, similarities and correspondences in sound and cadence and the frequency of their recurrence had also to be faithfully rendered. The result has been thus described by Mrs. Nelly Lautenberg of Ascona, Switzerland, to whom the present writer is indebted for these details: 'It is a version of unusual freshness and potency, one reads it as though reading the Hebrew Bible for the first time. To many this has proved a unique challenge and a most inspiring experience.' And the spoken word enshrined in Hebrew Scripture was no soliloquy. As

Jacob Agus wrote in his *Modern Philosophies of Judaism*, the Buber-Rosenzweig translation strove above all to render it as what it truly is, a revelatory dialogue between God and Israel.

So little is known outside the Jewish community about Buber's outstanding work for the Jews of Germany in the fateful years 1933–1938 that the 1964 printing of the *Encyclopaedia Britannica* even states that Buber left Germany when Hitler came to power.[10] The truth is otherwise. Already, in the spring of 1933, Buber suggested to the representative body of German Jewry that they establish a cultural institute for their people, not 'an emergency structure but a house to withstand all weathers'. It could have only one foundation: the Hebrew Bible. Before the dark year was out the Jewish Lehrhaus at Frankfurt, which had been closed soon after Rosenzweig's death, was reopened. A distinguished non-Jew[11] who was present at the courses Buber now gave there described them as 'historic events'. Another Lehrhaus was opened, at Stuttgart, as a centre from which Buber's influence could radiate. In May 1934 Buber summoned a conference on Jewish education at Herrlingen, near Ulm, and gave the opening address. 'Martin Buber', Ernst Simon has written,[12] 'stood at the centre of all this work. He held Bible courses on the most varied themes . . . For many people it was the first time they were brought face to face with the Bible. It was an experience that has lived with them for decades.'

It was also Ernst Simon, speaking at the Buber Memorial Seminar on Jewish-Arab Understanding at Tel Aviv in 1966, who said of his efforts in those years, 'Anyone who did not see Buber then has not seen true civil courage.' But at least we get memorable glimpses of him. At the close of 1933, Buber gave to students of the three German–Swiss universities an address in which he attacked the very life-basis of totalitarianism, and which was actually published in Germany in 1936. 'The fact that it could be published with impunity', Buber afterwards wrote,[13] 'is certainly to be explained from its not having been understood by the appropriate authorities.' But he had not waited until then to deliver to the Nazis a challenge that they could not fail to understand. In the autumn of 1934, Buber spoke at the Frankfurt Lehrhaus on 'The Power of the Spirit'.[14] He opposed to pagan glorification of the elemental powers of appetite, sex and the will to power, and to Christian subjugation of those powers, Jewish sanctification of them. When he courageously repeated this address in the Berlin Philharmonie, some two hundred S.S. men were among those who heard him declare:

> Heathenism glorifies elemental forces as such; they are considered sacred; they are declared holy, but not transformed . . . This glorification, this divine rank of theirs, cannot be maintained because the spirit which has empowered them cannot draw upon inexhaustible depths . . .
>
> In the 'reality system' of Judaism, the elemental forces are connected with the living faith in a union holy from time immemorial. Thus, blood and soil are hallowed in the promise made to Abraham, because they are bound up with the command to be 'a blessing' (Gen. 12:2). 'Seed' and 'earth' are promised, but only in order that—in the race of man scattered through the confusion of languages and divided into 'islands of the nations' (Gen. 10:5)—a new people may 'keep the way of the Lord to do righteousness and justice' (Gen. 18:19) in his land, and so begin building humanity.

It would be difficult to find, in Hitler's Germany or elsewhere, a more radical challenge to paganism, racialism and false nationalism. Buber was openly opposing to *Mein Kampf* his own *Kampf um Israel*. It was not possible that the 'appropriate authorities' should fail to understand this; they were not meant to. The Nazis immediately banned Buber from speaking in public or to closed meetings of Jewish organizations. A Frankfurt Quaker, at no small risk, gave him the opportunity to continue his lectures at closed sessions of non-Jewish organizations and Buber repeatedly did so.

He also found a way of reaching his wider Jewish public through the printed word, by what became known as the technique of 'the new Midrash'. In 1936, the firm of Schocken published Buber's pointed selection of twenty-three Psalms, under the title, taken from the first one, *Out of the depths have I cried unto Thee*.[15] It concludes with the inspiring last words of Psalm 57:

Awake, my glory; awake, psaltery and harp;
I will awake the dawn.
I will give thanks unto Thee, O Lord, among the peoples;
I will sing praises unto Thee among the nations.
For Thy mercy is great unto the heavens,
And Thy truth unto the skies.
Be Thou exalted, O God, above the heavens;
Thy glory be above all the earth.

Where others propounded the no-solution of an accelerated
assimilationism, or the Zionist political nationalism that was like
other nationalisms except that it seemed unattainable, Buber
offered the Jew only the Jewish spirit 'which time and again wells
up, streams, pours itself out, and settles. In short, man's bond
with God *which is always taking place*.'[16] In the opening words of
the first Schocken Almanac (1933–1934), Buber described the
Jew as 'inwardly the most exposed man in the world', the
man in whom the tensions of the epoch culminate in order
to measure their strength against him. For that most exposed
man of our time there was only one 'house able to withstand
all weathers'—the 'ancestral home' in which Buber took his
stand.

The most exposed man in the world, who suffers the tensions
of the epoch, is humanity's sacrifice to its hideous idols. The lives
of German Jewry were forfeit. Buber, now almost silenced, had
to witness a manifestation of 'human nature' without Biblical
parallel or historical precedent.[17] And at that moment the call
came to him to go to Jerusalem. A terrible decision confronted
him. His choice was the image of his life message: towards
Jerusalem. He delayed leaving Germany. He wanted to come to
Jerusalem on a tourist's visa, to be free to return if he was
needed. But he obeyed the summons.

*   *   *

'Buber', writes Eliyahu Honig,[18] 'can be justly regarded as one
of the founding pioneers of the Hebrew University of Jerusalem.'
As far back as 1902 he had, with Berthold Feiwel and Chaim
Weizmann, written a pamphlet appealing for *Eine Jüdische
Hochschule*. This and the efforts of the Zionist Organization
resulted in 1911 in a programme of action which was presented

to the Tenth Zionist Congress. The decision to establish a University was taken at the 1913 Zionist Congress in Vienna. Nevertheless, there were objections from the University's Board of Governors to the appointment of Buber, which were overcome by its first President, Dr. J. L. Magnes. The Chair of Social Philosophy was probably a compromise, but nobody could have doubted what Social Philosophy—or rather philosophical anthropology—would become in the hands of this man.

His first address, delivered a little more than a month after Hitler had marched into his native Vienna, was the first of a series, 'What is Man?'[19] The epigraph was from Rousseau and the lecture took up Kant's final all-inclusive question. But at that juncture and in Jerusalem it could hardly fail to recall also the terrible lament of Job:

> Therefore I will not refrain my mouth;
> I will speak in the anguish of my spirit;
> I will complain in the bitterness of my soul.
> Am I a sea, or a sea-monster,
> That Thou settest a watch over me?
> When I say 'My bed shall comfort me,
> My couch shall ease my complaint';
> Then Thou scarest me with dreams,
> And terrifiest me through visions;
> So that my soul chooseth strangling,
> And death rather than these my bones.
> I loathe it; I shall not live alway;
> Let me alone; for my days are vanity.
> *What is man*, that Thou shouldest magnify him,
> And that Thou shouldest remember him every morning,
> And try him every moment?
> How long wilt Thou not look away from me,
> Nor let me alone till I swallow down my spittle?   [men?
> If I have sinned, what do I unto Thee, O Thou watcher of
> Why hast Thou set me as mark for Thee,
> So that I am a burden to myself?
> And why dost Thou not pardon my transgression,
> And take away mine iniquity?
> For now shall I lie down in the dust;
> And Thou wilt seek me, but I shall not be.

Then he wrote the Hasidic chronicle *Gog and Magog* (*For the Sake of Heaven*) in which a sage torn between the unbearableness of human suffering and longing to behold its cessation attempts by desperate magic to convert the wars of Napoleon into the final struggle that was to precede the coming of the Messiah. 'Fully to understand this passage', he says elsewhere,[20] in indicating its central theme, 'the reader must recall the time at which the novel was written.' It was 1940.

Then came the direct appeal to the Hebrew Bible. It was as though he too had to go down before the cruel inquisition of the War in Europe, from the level of direct address to the twentieth century by a contemporary—in 'What is Man?'—to the Hasidic islands of life and hope in the Europe that was now being destroyed forever—in *For the Sake of Heaven*—to the bedrock of the Bible itself. He had written one important volume of Biblical interpretation while still at work on the Bible translation in Germany: *Königtum Gottes*, in 1931, enlarged in 1936, from which Friedman quotes these now doubly significant words:[21] 'The Man in the Israelite world who has faith is not distinguished from the "heathen" by a more spiritual view of the Godhead, but by the exclusiveness of his relationship to God and by his reference of all things to Him.' Now followed *The Teaching of the Prophets* (*The Prophetic Faith*), 1942, and the great *Moses*, in 1944. The iron hand in Europe had closed on his people. There is a passage[22] in *The Prophetic Faith* which shows how he neither conceals nor exhibits his own deepest experience, how indeed, as he had declared in Germany in 1933, nothing could separate him from the sacred history of his people. Each sober word is written in blood:

> From the moment when a national disaster appears inevitable, and especially after it has become a reality, it can, like every great torment, become a productive force from the religious point of view: it begins to suggest new questions and to stress old ones. Dogmatized conceptions are pondered afresh in the light of the events, and the faith relationship that has to stand the test of an utterly changed situation is renewed in a modified form. But the new acting force is nothing less than the force of extreme despair, a despair so elemental that it can have but one of two results.

The sapping of the last will of life, or the renewal of the soul.

But where, as in the final speech of what was perhaps Shakespeare's final play, the absolutes of despair and prayer are equipoised, despair is denied its ultimate absoluteness. There is no real contradiction between the passage just cited and the spontaneous response with which Dr. Malcolm L. Diamond concludes his book.[23] Buber had been asked, if Israel was so far from the Israel of his vision, why did it not cause him to despair? Buber leaned forward: 'Despair! Despair! In the darkest days of our history I did not despair and I certainly do not despair now!'

Other important Biblical works soon followed. The slowly matured and crucial interpretation of the Adam myth in Genesis: *Images of Good and Evil*, and the brief but vital book on the Psalms, *Right and Wrong*, in which Buber expresses the view on personal survival that most of his commentators pass over in silence. The important essay 'Abraham the Seer' came somewhat later.

Buber had long contended for Jewish–Arab friendship, to the length of proposing against the great majority of Jewish opinion a bi-national state in Palestine. But scarcely was the World War over than Jew was fighting Arab on the soil of the Holy Land itself, Jerusalem was invested and 'during the days of its so-called siege, or rather in the chaos of destruction which broke out within it',[24] Buber began without plan but completed the book in which he penetrates to the heart of the New Testament and reclaims Jesus for Judaism, *Two Types of Faith*. But before this his whole vision of Hasidism had been transfigured too. The exquisite volumes of *Tales of the Hasidim* appeared, and the anthology of Hasidic sayings, *Ten Rungs*. 'Along with much else', Buber wrote,[25] 'I owe the urge to this new and more comprehensive composition to the air of this land. Our sages say that it makes one wise; to me it has granted a different gift; the strength to make a new beginning. I had regarded my work on the hasidic legends as completed . . .'

His life-work was not yet complete. He had interpreted the message of Moses and the Prophets, of Genesis and the Psalms. In 1951, at the age of seventy-three, Buber retired from the Hebrew University and settled in Jerusalem to take up his translation into German of the Hebrew Bible once more. The Bible still had absolute priority over his own compositions. Friedman's foreword to the last volume of Buber's philosophical anthropology, *The Knowledge of Man*, begins thus:

> It has been eleven years since Martin Buber and I met with the Religious Book department of Harper's to discuss the plans for Professor Buber's forthcoming philosophical anthropology: his study of the problem of man. Because of his great work translating the Hebrew Bible into German and because of the thousand other demands on his time, Professor Buber told me then that it would be a matter of grace if he were allowed to finish his anthropology. This grace was given him.[26]

And Friedman was able to end his 1963 translation of one of Buber's early works[27] with the simple statement: 'Honoured throughout the world, Martin Buber has recently completed the translation of the Bible into German which he and Rosenzweig began almost forty years ago.'

But even the Bible translation could not prevent Buber from taking, in the new state of Israel, the sort of direct teaching action which had been his response to the rise of the Nazis in Germany. At a University Conference in London in 1924 he had lectured on his plan for a Popular School for Higher Studies to be attached to the future Hebrew University. Yet it was only in the new State, under the terrible pressure of mass immigration and the need for adult education, that his plan was implemented. The Seminar for Adult Educators was set up in 1949 and directed by Buber, even after his retirement from the University, until 1953, with the help of Dr. Gideon Freudenberg. In the University's Year Book for 1950, Buber wrote on 'A New Venture in Adult Education'. That it was once more the 'house to withstand all weathers' is clear from its conclusion:[28]

> ... care should be taken to avoid all isolated consideration in the study of Jewish history, contemporary Jewish affairs, Hebrew language and literature, and Jewish sociology and knowledge of Palestine. Our great national treasure for which there is no substitute is our prophetic universality; the kind of nationalism that sets apart, that isolates, is alien

to the spirit and true essence of Israel. If we take the latter course, it will lead us to the decisive kind of assimilation, to assimilation as a nation. Furthermore, we shall not be able to bring about a true bond between the masses of new-comers to the country and our national regeneration, unless we link them to its basic and vital tradition, which is constantly being renewed and which endures by virtue of the new values it creates. This we cannot do unless we combine that tradition with the great tradition of the human spirit, with the struggle of the spirit for eternal values. Living Judaism can only be taught in such a manner as to restore faith in the meaning of the world and of life to those who have lost it.

In 1952, Buber received the Goethe Prize at the University of Hamburg, and in the following year the Peace Prize of the German Book Trade at Frankfurt am Main. His acceptance of this prize and his decision to go to Germany to receive it aroused a storm of protest among Jews everywhere. His opening words on this occasion must be cited in full:

> I cannot express my thanks to the German Book Trade for the honour conferred on me without at the same time setting forth the sense in which I have accepted it, just as I earlier acepted the Hanseatic Goethe Prize given me by the University of Hamburg.
>
> About a decade ago a considerable number of Germans—there must have been many thousands of them—under the indirect command of the German government and the direct command of its representatives, killed millions of my people in a systematically prepared and executed procedure whose organized cruelty cannot be compared with any previous historical event. I, who am one of those who remained alive, have only in a formal sense a common humanity with those who took part in this action. They have so radically removed themselves from the human sphere, so transposed themselves into a sphere of monstrous inhumanity inaccessible to my conception, that not even hatred, much less an overcoming of hatred, was able to arise in me. And what am I that I could here presume to 'forgive'!

With the German people it is otherwise. From my youth on I have taken the real existence of peopels most seriously. But I never, in the face of any historical moment, past or present, allowed the concrete multiplicity existing at that moment within a people—the concrete inner dialectic, rising to contradiction—to be obscured by the levelling concept of a totality constituted and acting in just such a way and no other.

When I think of the German people of the days of Auschwitz and Treblinka, I behold, first of all, the great many who knew that the monstrous event was taking place and did not oppose it. But my heart, which is acquainted with the weakness of men, refuses to condemn my neighbour for not prevailing upon himself to become a martyr. Next there emerges before me the mass of those who remained ignorant of what was withheld from the German public, and who did not try to discover what reality lay behind the rumours which were circulating. When I have these men in mind, I am gripped by the thought of the anxiety, likewise well known to me, of the human creature before a truth which he fears he cannot face. But finally there appears before me, from reliable reports, some who have become as familiar to me by sight, action, and voice as if they were friends, those who refused to carry out the orders and suffered death or put themselves to death, and those who learned what was taking place and opposed it and were put to death, or those who learned what was taking place and because they could do nothing to stop it killed themselves. I see these men very near before me in that especial intimacy which binds us at times to the dead and to them alone. Reverence and love for these Germans now fills my heart.[29]

It is not so much an error as a sympton of the drama of our time that Dr. Diamond, summarizing this speech in his book,[30] reverses the order of the groups and makes Buber seem to move from praise of the righteous Germans to indictment of the wicked. But the movement of Buber's Judaism was in the opposite direction. In this acid test of his Hasidic faith he still sought to pierce the thick armour, the 'shells' of totalitarian reality and to liberate the precious 'sparks' that persisted even there, to find the human point at which the relation between Jew and German, between man and man, could again become that between an I and a Thou. And the title of *Ich und Du*, written in Germany thirty years before had surely also appealed to the archetype of human brotherhood in the spirit. It was Jonathan who said to David, 'And as touching the matter which I and thou have spoken of, behold the LORD is between me and thee for ever.' (I Sam. 20:23). Not something like 'And may God bless our friendship' but 'behold' and 'is'. And as his crowning work Buber had gone on to complete the gift of the Hebrew Bible to the German people in their own tongue.

* * *

Martin Buber was far from imagining that the Bible can communicate easily with its readers:

> Since this book came into being, it has confronted generation after generation. Each generation must struggle with the Bible in its turn, and come to terms with it. The generations are by no means always ready to listen to what the book has to say, and to obey it; they are often vexed and defiant; nevertheless, the preoccupation with this book is part of their life and they face it in the realm of reality. Even when generations negated the Book, the very negation confirmed the Book's claim upon them: they bore witness to the Book in the very act of denying it.[31]

But perhaps it has never been more difficult than it is for the man of today, in this age of what Buber calls the eclipse of God, though not the absence of God:

> The man of today has no access to a sure and solid faith, nor can it be made accessible to him. If he examines himself seriously, he knows this and may not delude himself further. But he is not denied the possibility of holding himself open to faith. If he is really serious, he too can open up to this book and let its rays strike him where they will. He can give himself up and submit to the test without preconceived notions and without reservations. He can absorb the Bible with all his strength, and wait to see what will happen to him, whether he will not discover within himself a new and

unbiased approach to this or that element in the book. But to this end, he must read the Jewish Bible as though it were something entirely unfamiliar, as though it had not been set before him ready-made, at school and after in the light of 'religious' and 'scientific' certainties; as though he has not been confronted all his life with sham concepts and sham statements which cited the Bible as their authority. He must face the book with a new attitude as something new. He must yield to it, withhold nothing of his being, and let whatever will occur between himself and it. He does not know which of its sayings and images will overwhelm him and mould him, from where the spirit will ferment and enter into him, to incorporate itself anew in his body. But he holds himself open. He does not believe anything *a priori*. He reads aloud[32] the words written in the book in front of him: he hears the word he utters and it reaches him. Nothing is prejudged. The current of time flows on, and the contemporary character of this man becomes itself a receiving vessel.[33]

* * *

A few weeks before Buber's death on 13 June 1965, in his eighty-eighth year, there was found among his papers what is taken to be his last poem, written in German in October 1964. The following translation by Maurice Friedman will appear, with the German text and notes on two untranslatable instances of word-play, in his edition of Martin Buber's *Gleanings: A Believing Humanism*:[34]

The Fiddler

Here on the world's edge at this hour I have
Wondrously settled my life.
Behind me in a boundless circle
The All is silent, only that fiddler fiddles.
Dark one, already I stand in covenant with you,
Ready to learn from your tones
Wherein I became guilty without knowing it.
Let me feel, let there be revealed
To this hale soul each wound
That I have incorrigibly inflicted and remained in illusion.
Do not stop, holy player, before then!

The *Jerusalem Post* remarked that the poem was 'evidently intended as his farewell to life' and it is at least clear that Buber had felt some cessation of the address of the Eternal Thou as command upon him. An obituary in *World Jewry*[35] observed that Buber was 'a sage and prophet not altogether honoured in his own country and by his own people'. But when towards the end of April 1965 Buber fell and fractured a hip amends were made. Almost simultaneously it was proposed to grant him the Freedom of Jerusalem, the motion was passed by a split vote of the municipal council in May and at the beginning of June, only ten days before Buber's death, the Mayor of Jerusalem called on him to convey the decision. After a brief lying-in-state in front of the University campus, the first pall-bearers were the President, the Prime Minister, the President of the University and the distinguished Hebrew author S. Y. Agnon. The funeral ceremony began with a eulogy by the Prime Minister, Levi Eshkol, who said:[36]

> The passing of Mordecai Martin Buber marks the end of an era in the annals of the spiritual and territorial resurgence of the Jewish people in modern times. The Jewish people today mourns a luminary and a teacher, a man of thought and achievement, who revealed the soul of Judaism with a new philosophic force. All mankind mourns with us one of the spiritual giants of this century. I do not know whether there is anyone else in our midst, in the sphere of spiritual life, who was so much a part of the heritage of the entire world; but he was deeply anchored—to a depth that few could reach—in his Jewishness, in the Jewish people, in the resurgence of Israel and the love of Jewry.

Whatever had been his differences with strictly observant Jews or too strictly political Zionists, now at last it was seen to be true that, in his own words, 'Nothing can separate me from the sacred history of Israel.'[37] Nor from the land to which he had come home. In the year Martin Buber was born in Vienna, 1878, the first new Hebrew village was set up in Palestine, Petach Tikva, east of Tel Aviv. The soil in which he rests is now once more Israel. It is fitting that among the memorials to him is one that will continue to put forth new leaf, a Martin Buber Forest.

THE WANDERER: ADAM

ADAM is myth. We do not understand myth. We do not trust it. It is not wanted in either of the 'two cultures'. It is not precisely factual statement devoid of all emotion. It is not aesthetic fantasy, with or without a deliberate 'message'.

In religion, as defined by dogma, doctrine, precept and law it is the problem child if not the illegitimate. The talk is much of 'demythologizing' religion.

We cannot proceed, we cannot begin to appreciate the teaching of the Hebrew tradition as apprehended by Martin Buber, without a glance at the modern status of the word 'myth'.

In popular usage, influenced by the rise of science, 'myth' has become the antithesis of 'truth'; or, perhaps much influenced by psychoanalysis, for distortion and disguise of a 'truth' that can finally be better stated in non-mythical terms. The general reader may therefore be alienated at the outset by Buber's emphasis on myth as the very fountain-head of living religion and as the primal form which it is strictly impossible to 'get behind'. Here we can only hope to bring the vital issue a little more into focus.

'Myth' is by no means a synonym for untruth among scientists who scarcely take Buber's view of its significance. 'As long ago as 1926, Malinowski could write of myth as "a vital ingredient of human civilization . . . not an intellectual explanation or an artistic imagery, but a pragmatic charter of primitive faith and moral wisdom".'[1] A recent article on the philosophical anthropology of Claude Levi-Strauss remarks that 'the idea that music and myth are akin, that they build shapes of being more universal, more numinous than speech, haunts the western imagination'.[2] It is, to say the least, premature to assume that the scientific investigation of myth will have found an ultimate answer if it can presently give an account of myth in terms of human brain-structure. The metaphysical question of what the brain is responding to remains and the religious submission is that this is the Creator who must remain, by definition, inconceivable to the creature.

In recent religious writing Buber is not alone in his emphasis on myth, despite the contrary rationalizing tendency. The work of Teilhard de Chardin has prompted the remark that 'in a day when it simply may not be possible to find an objective language to mediate the truths of religion and science, we might still hope for a myth which would say more about reality than can be spoken in dispassionate terms, yet communicate it to us in accents unmistakably our own. Is Teilhard then the great re-mythologizer of our time?'[3] And the Protestant theologian Paul Tillich, who may well have been influenced by Buber in this, writes (in 'The Religious Symbol', a paper circulated to the Fourth Annual Meeting of the New York Institute of Philosophy, in whose symposium Tillich participated; see *Religious Experience and Truth*, ed. Sidney Hook, 1962, pp. 310, 320) that 'Yahweh acquires the unconditionedness which is intended in the religious act. But the myth is not thereby removed . . . If it (the uncon-ditioned transcendence) is to be perceived—and it must be so in religion—it can be done only in mythical conceptions . . . The highest concept or even an abstractly transcendent mysticism has necessarily a mythical element still within it.' Of the essen-tially mythic character of scientific concepts he says, '. . . in the most highly educated circles the attitude of certainty towards scientific concepts is shattered and . . . the mythical character of these concepts is recognized'.

In rabbinical Judaism, Maimonidean 'rationalism' tends to preponderate. This recently led one authority to say, with reference to Franz Rosenzweig, whose teaching he was criticizing: 'One of the finest creations of the human mind to aid the spread of false doctrines and superstitious belief is the myth . . .'[4] Gershom Scholem, speaking of medieval Jewish philosophy, says that 'Judaism strove to open up a region, that of monotheistic revelation, from which mythology would be excluded . . . the tendency of the classical Jewish tradition (is) to liquidate myth as a central spiritual power'.[5] But Scholem wisely observes that this tends to preserve the purity of the concept of God at the cost of His living reality and, treating of the reappearance of myth in the Kabbalah, asserts, 'Equally pronounced and significant for the history of Judaism was the restoration of the mythical character of the Torah.'[6] Finally it should be noted that when Yehezkel Kaufman speaks of 'the absence of myth'[7]—in his monumental study of the religion of Israel—he means by 'myth' stories of the birth, loves and wars of deities as found in pagan religion. Kaufman uses 'legend' for what Buber means by 'myth'—stories which reflect within the modes and limitations of human faculties man's encounter with the divine.

The general status of 'myth' in Biblical studies is perhaps best indicated by the following words, printed in bold type in the article on Genesis by Professor S. H. Hooke, in the new (1962) completely revised edition of *Peake's Commentary on the Bible* (§ 144a): 'a myth can, and often does, represent a kind of truth which cannot be expressed in historical categories.'

The general problem of the relevance of myth to modern man is well expressed in an article ('Myths for Moderns' TLS. 10.2.66, p. 102) on the work of the eminent historian of religions, Mircea Eliade, who ascribes the 'tragic existence' of modern man to 'a process of desacralization'.

Man is haunted by realities that he has denied, and his earlier religious behaviour is still present emotionally in his deepest being 'ready to be reactualized'. It is easy to demonstrate this from the superstitions and taboos of modern man, his 'camouflaged myths and degenerate rituals'; New Year festivities, house-warming ceremonies, marriage rites and parties at the birth of a child or a social advancement. The myths of modern man appear in the plays he enjoys, the books he reads, the cinema ('that dream factory'), and television; with fights between heroes and monsters, paradisal landscapes and descents into hell. Even reading fulfils a mythological function, because it enables man to 'escape from time', as in so many ancient rituals. To 'kill time' with a detective story introduces the reader into another world outside personal duration and change, and makes him live another history, a foretaste of immortality.

The mythological structure of communism has often been remarked, with its eschatological content and redeeming role of the just, taken over from the great eschatological myths of the Asian-Mediterranean world. But lower levels and 'little religions' may also show degenerate religious behaviour; nudism and movements for complete sexual freedom reveal 'a nostalgia for Eden', a myth of the paradisal state of man before the Fall. In business and in war, in exploits and in psychoanalysis, modern man 'without religion' still holds on to pseudo-religions and degenerate mythologies. This is inevitable because he is fed by impulses that come from the 'depths of his being'. 'A purely rational man is an abstraction; he is never found in real life.' But the tragedy of modern man is that his private mythologies never rise to the true status of myths, just because they are private and are not experienced by the whole man. Although they are experiences in dream or imagination, these private myths do not, as myths do in the great religions, provide a world-view and a solid basis for a system of behaviour. In other words, modern man is nourished by the myths of the unconscious, but he does not thereby achieve a truly religious experience or vision of the world. This non-religion is equivalent to a new 'fall' of man; he does not understand the role of religion and hence cannot live it consciously.

Before endeavouring to follow Buber into the field of Biblical myth and Hasidic tale we must fully grasp the fact that this is for him the basic category, subsidiary to no other kind of 'explanation', the only possible form of report of human experiences of the highest value, something that we remove into another and alien category when we submit it to intellectual analysis and explanatory comment.

'The fundamental attitude of Jewish religiosity and the core of that Jewish monotheism which has been so vastly misunderstood, so cruelly rationalized, is to regard all things as manifestations of God, all events as a revelation of the Absolute . . .' 'We must call myth any narrative of a simply real event in which this event is felt and represented as divine.' Myth is 'the inspiring source of all true religiosity', it is 'the living force of the Jewish experience of God'. 'If it remains possible that by reverencing the divine according to our individual feeling, we may still hear the wing-beats of the Jewish spirit, it is the sublime power of our myth that we have to thank for it.'[8]

The impulse to demythologize religion is not of recent origin.

It is as old as the Bible itself, indeed as old as man. Twelve years before he set himself to the immense task of translating the Bible, Buber spoke of its composition. Accepting the essential findings of modern Biblical scholarship, he believes that the Bible was cast into the form in which we possess it by a body of men inspired by the spirit of the official late Jewish priesthood who looked upon myth as 'the natural enemy of religion as they conceived it, and accordingly removed everything of a mythical nature from the abundance of written records that had come down to them. Fortunately, the knowledge of this priesthood was limited, and certain elements of whose original character they were unaware, were allowed to slip through. And thus we find scattered through every book of the Bible veins of pure ore.'[9]

What comes to each of us in everyday experience of the here and now is inexpressible, it is pregnant with divine significance. The shape we give to it in thoughts and words is our individual limitation of the illimitable, valuable insofar as it preserves and intimates its divine origin, inimical insofar as it is accepted as definitive of the indefinable, or as over-riding the ever-new appearances in which the unseen divinity uniquely manifests itself to the individual.

Of course, myth can be perverted into fiction. How then may we distinguish between false myth and true? Myth is to be verified by search—governed neither by the concepts and standards of psychological analysis nor by those of sociological doctrines or norms—of the mystery of the self. 'The myth is an eternal function of the soul.' 'Each living man is rooted in living myth.'[10] Already we begin to glimpse something of what is implicit in the words Buber later addressed to the man of today faced with the Bible, which were quoted in the Introduction: 'He must yield to it, withhold nothing of his being, and let whatever will occur between himself and it. He does not know which of its sayings and images will overwhelm him and mould him, from where the spirit will ferment and enter into him, to incorporate itself anew in his body. But he holds himself open.'

* * *

The second verse of the Hebrew Bible follows so strangely upon the first that an unprejudiced reader is at once taken off his guard. 'In the beginning God created the heaven and the earth'

—the first sentence has lost for most of us the stupendous character of its plain assertion. But if, as the pious say, God is good, surely we shall next read that the earth He created was good? No. 'The earth was unformed and void,' or, as Buber renders it,[11] 'in a state of confusion and desolation.'

This 'confusion and desolation' was not then abandoned by its Creator. 'Darkness was upon the face of the deep,' but 'the spirit of God hovered over the face of the waters.' God said, 'let there be light' and there was light. 'And God saw the light, that it was good.'

We need to remind ourselves that this was written down by a man, whether Moses or another. He was trying to articulate his image of the beginning of all things, of a time before man was. If we reject, as Buber does, the idea of verbal inspiration that would reduce the writer to something like a trance medium speaking automatically, but nevertheless do not dismiss the implications of 'inspiration' and 'revelation', we must accept this as a supreme human effort to express the inexpressible and realize that the writer was drawing on the soundless depths of his own nature to describe the birth of all nature.

He speaks of the earth—from which Man was formed—as a formless void, a something that is also somehow nothing. Of a hovering divine spirit of which no image is possible. Of the 'light' that God commanded to shine forth. And this light is 'good'. Nothing is formed before this 'light' or without it.

We must attempt to translate that account into terms of the human nature of the writer. Man, the quintessence of dust, is free—and freedom is in itself a formless void. Where all things are possible nothing is actual. However urgently motivated may be the movements made only out of that void they are random movements—wandering. They lead to nothing. Form does not emerge.

But when a man turns his whole self to the imageless reality whose presence is vouchsafed by the light—a manifestation of God through his creation but not God Himself—and freely chooses to follow wheresoever it leads—for it is not, or not only, within him—formation takes place, his true 'I' comes into being, his movement can be whole and purposeful, he chooses *the* way.

Something like what this is meant to indicate, we may suppose, has been Martin Buber's own experience, something like this is his reading of the Hebrew Bible, with some such primeval reference he writes, 'always there are, not left and right, but the vortex of chaos and the spirit hovering over it. Of the two paths, one is a setting out upon no path, pseudo-decision which is indecision, flight into delusion and ultimately into mania; the other is the path, for there is only one.'[12]

One, that is, for each man. Each unique person has his own unique and largely private way which only he can follow in each unique moment. To follow it is Good. To wander from it is Evil.

*   *   *

Adam is the wanderer.[13] On him is conferred freedom unlimited except by human limitation. Wherever he turns, whatever he does, he may be following the light that leads him on the way. What he must not attempt to do is to usurp the prerogative of leadership, to be God himself and to determine his way in that light which is only the reflection of himself. He must not attempt to be what he is not, Creator as well as creature. The prohibition, or perhaps we may say the warning of the impossibility and of the fatal consequences of disregarding it, has its single visible sign in the world, and the Law yet consists only of the commandment relating to it: 'Of every tree of the garden thou mayest freely eat; but of the tree of the knowledge of good and evil, thou shalt not eat of it; for in the day that thou eatest thereof thou shalt surely die.' The true knowledge of good *and* evil, the ultimate truth in which the things of time find their true accounting in the order of eternity, is shared by God only with those 'other celestial beings' who are 'subject to Him and without names or power of their own'.[14]

The way is open only to the man who devotes himself wholly to it. Wandering is the fate of the man who allows some part or impulse to predominate over the wholeness, which thus ceases to exist at all for that time. Perhaps something of this is obscurely imaged in the strange report that Eve was formed from one of Adam's ribs. Certainly it is when this 'part become a whole' takes an initiative unknown to Adam that wandering first comes upon them both. But the 'part become a whole' does not deliberately revolt against the commandment. It succumbs to a dream of God-like knowledge.

The serpent-tempter is an enigmatic figure. 'It speaks,' says

Buber, 'as though it knew very imprecisely what it obviously knows very precisely'. Not, as the standard translation of the Masoretic text[15] has it, in the form of a question—'Yea, hath God said: Ye shall not eat of any tree of the garden?'—but, as Buber translates,[16] in an unfinished sentence of insinuation: 'Indeed, God has said: You shall not eat of every tree of the garden . . .'

Eve follows suit, exaggerating the prohibition to '. . . touch it not, else you must die.' It is only necessary to add a misleading gloss to the divine words and the way is lost. The tempter can now securely offer a show of pure reason on his side: if God's pre-eminence rests on His knowledge of good and evil; and if eating the fruit of this tree confers that knowledge on the eater; then it follows that the eater achieves the same immortality as the deity; and the threat of death is exposed as mere bluff on the part of a God who is only jealous of His precarious superiority. 'Ye shall not surely die . . .' (Genesis 3:4).

If we bear in mind the writer, and also the non-conceptual character of myth, we shall see the single whole man in whose 'sleep' a part becomes autonomous; the whole man then disappears from the scene for a while and the part succumbs to a temptation to be greater than the whole, by drifting away from reality and by heeding a plausible rationalization. Now imagination is free to go beyond the direct evidence of experience. 'The woman regards the tree. She does not merely see that it is a delight to the eye, she also sees in it that which cannot be seen: how good its fruit tastes and that it bestows the gift of understanding.'[17] Buber will not concede that 'seeing' here means 'perceiving'—how could the 'gift of understanding' be perceived before the fruit was tasted? He calls Eve's 'seeing' 'a strange, dreamlike kind of contemplation'.[18] The passive acceptance of the fruit by the silent Adam whose presence is only now revealed is 'dream-lassitude'.[19] There is no Lucifer-like rebellion; perhaps there is what is now sometimes called wishful thinking. But in that sense, at least, we may accept Buber's comment: 'It is apparent; the two doers know not what they do.'[20]

What are the consequences? The serpent was both right and wrong, says Buber,[21] in denying that death would follow. 'They do not have to die after eating, they merely plunge into *human* mortality, that is, into the knowledge of death to come.' Perhaps one might say that from awareness of infinitude in all things,

including themselves, they change to awareness of finitude in all
things, including themselves, and of a condition that may be
called fragmentariness. Everything has its conflicting purposes
and its inexorable limitation, including their own lives. How far
that is presented by the Hebrew Bible as final truth about
mortality we shall consider later.

Buber discerns deep irony in the Genesis story of Adam and
Eve and the crowning irony is in the words attributed to God:
'Behold, the man (not, it may be noted, the man and the woman)
is become as one of us, to know good and evil . . .' The gulf
between Creator and creature is not closed, any more than
communication between them is finally broken. God's knowledge
of good and evil remains one thing. Man's 'knowledge' of good
and evil is necessarily and tragically other.

> God knows the opposites of being, which stem from His own
> act of creation; He encompasses them, untouched by them;
> He is absolutely familiar with them as He is absolutely
> superior to them; He has direct intercourse with them . . .
> and this in their function as the opposite poles of the world's
> being. For as such He created them—we may impute this
> late Biblical doctrine (Isaiah 45:7) to our narrator, in its
> elementary form.[22]

But 'a superior-familiar encompassing of opposites is denied' to
man

> who, despite his 'likeness' to God, has a part only in that
> which is created and not in creation, is capable only of
> begetting and giving birth, not of creating. Good and evil,
> the yes-position and the no-position of existence, enter into
> his living cognizance; but in him they can never be tem-
> porally co-existent. He knows oppositeness only by his
> situation within it; and that means *de facto* (since the yes can
> present itself to the experience and perception of man in the
> no-position but not the no in the yes-position).[23]

There is divine compassion in the stern retribution that leads
God to follow his acknowledgment that man has 'become as one
of us to know good and evil' with the sending forth of Adam and
Eve from Eden, so that they should not take also of the tree of
life 'and live for ever'. A period is set to this situation within the

oppositeness of good and evil. Now the way must be found in the history of a world in which 'the opposites which are always latently present in creation break out into actual reality, they become existent'.[24]

From the union of the primal pair who seized on the human alternating knowledge of good and evil spring a pair of contrasted sons, Cain and Abel. These must not be simply identified with Evil and Good, but we hear nothing of Abel except his submission to God's will and almost nothing of Cain but his disastrous lapse into wrong-doing. It is this side of Adam's nature that tends, as it were, to be first and foremost. Cain slays Abel and becomes 'a fugitive and a wanderer in the earth' (Genesis 4:12). We hear nothing of any offspring of Abel.

In Buber's view, the story of Cain's crime does not bring us into the presence of full-fledged evil. True, Adam's choice was disobedience by an act not otherwise wrong in itself, and Cain's choice is one 'which if, as here, it took place within the clan, would always be punished as such in every society known to us'.[25] But this is the *first* human killing and Cain, like Adam and Eve, does not *know* what it is he does. However much experience other men have had, this is still to some extent true of every 'first' killing. The English priest, in Shaw's *St. Joan*, insists on burning the prisoner, but after seeing this done he wanders in his mind. Buber rightly gives full weight to what the Bible understands by 'knowledge'. This is not 'theory' it is the full intimacy of real experience. Truly Cain, like his father, cannot 'know' what he does until he has done it. To God's question and sentence beginning 'What hast thou done,' Cain replies 'My punishment is greater than I can bear.' (Genesis 4:10–12.)

Buber's contention that Cain strikes 'in the vortex of indecision'[26] is his attempt to locate a frontier between what he calls the first stage and the second stage of Evil, a distinction between inadvertent sin and deliberate wickedness. Nevertheless, the transition is fatally easy—'Intensification and confirmation of indecision is decision to evil.'[27] This second stage can, of course, occur in the individual. But both stages occur also in human groups and societies and we may conveniently defer consideration of the deliberate choice of the way that is no way to the next chapter, on the generations before and after Noah.

What must be emphasized here is that the Hebrew myth of

Adam is not, like the Christian interpretation of it, a doctrine of a
'Fall' in which all mankind is inescapably involved, and it is not
essentially a matter of sexuality, however much the departure
from the way of free acceptance of the divine will affects even,
and especially, this most intimate of all human relations. Man
'sins as Adam sinned and not because Adam sinned'.[28] Man is
made 'in the divine image'. He cannot, as Adam wished, become
like God. He cannot, as the hardened rebel supposes, be God,
his own God. But there is yet the true *imitatio Dei*. 'The Fall of the
first human being consisted in his wanting to reach the likeness
intended for him in his creation by other means than by perfect-
ing "the image".'[29] The true way is, as the hundredth Psalm was
once interpreted: 'toward Him we perfect our souls.'[30] By
following the way.

*   *   *

Only when there was a human pair did the 'wandering' begin.
Only when they had grown into a family was the first act wrong
in itself committed. Both the wandering and the way lie across
the realm of relationships, in society and in history. But in the
Bible the human myth of the beginning first shows us man alone
(alone, but hearing the divine command) and although Hasidism, to which we now turn, is very much a community movement, we are concerned in this chapter with what, in Buber's
interpretation, it has to say to us about the individual. Already,
in the preface to *Images of Good and Evil*, the book in which he
considers the myth of Adam, Buber gives his reply to the
question, at what point must the struggle against evil begin: 'The
struggle must begin within one's own soul—all else will follow
upon this,' and goes on directly to refer to his elaboration of that
answer in his Hasidic chronicle tale, *For the Sake of Heaven*. And
his small, sublimely simple but important work, *The Way of Man
According to the Teaching of Hasidism*, includes a chapter entitled
'Beginning With Oneself'.

This little book opens with a Hasidic tale about Adam, of which
that maxim is the 'moral'. Indeed, all six sections of it begin with
and contain such Hasidic tales, or 'legends', as they are most
often called, since an element of the marvellous is often present in
the tradition as it was orally communicated by generations before
being written down. This element of the marvellous should not

be misunderstood. It is to be regarded less as pious fiction than as an attempt to convey how, as Buber said of Biblical myth, a simply real event is felt and represented as divine. The marvellous tries to arouse that inexpressible sense of the divine which was present in the original experience.

Buber has been criticized[31] for concentrating too much on the legendary material of Hasidism, at the expense of the also very extensive 'doctrinal' literature. Rabbi Shneur Zalman, for instance, the hero of the first tale in *The Way of Man*, himself wrote an important doctrinal work which can now be read in English.[32] But Buber's selection of Hasidic tales[33] does not stand alone. He has also written extensively about the origins, life and teaching of the movement.[34] His emphasis on the legends, however, is to be understood in the light of his attitude to myth as (we have already noted) 'the inspiring source of all true religiosity', 'the living force of the Jewish experience of God', the quintessential element in the Hebrew Bible and the soil in which is rooted each living man.

Moreover, techniques—as distinct from exemplary patterns and hallowed traditions—of prayer and meditation are as repugnant to him as deliberate tactics in intimate human relations are to many of us. The idea that it is possible or desirable to evolve standard methods whereby one could 'make friends and influence' the deity is not less questionable, surely, than the same sort of notion applied to our dealings with those dearest to us. Also, though Hasidism did vital work in taking up much of the conceptual structure of the Kabbalah and purifying that extraordinary mystical tradition of elements of gnosis and magic while retaining much of its vocabulary and imagery, it is significant not as a source of 'new' doctrinal ideas but as a way of living together, as a revitalized manifestation of embryonic social cells of the holy Hebrew nation, the people covenanted to God. In that life what counts most is not doctrine or technique, or even pedantic dispute about the niceties of the Law, but the spontaneous response of the unique person in a unique situation in which a spark is waiting to be struck into life. That is why we often need to know the situation, the 'story', to appreciate the words that welled up from its depths. Hasidic aphorisms[35] are sometimes generalized 'wisdom' but are often the finding, in something that just unpredictably happens, of a heart of meaning and value that, just because it is the heart of the matter, speaks also to other men and their occasions.

The tale that opens *The Way of Man* is told of Rabbi Shneur Zalman, in prison awaiting trial, of whom the chief of police begins to ask, for the sake of argument and testing his captive rather than for enlightenment, difficult questions about the Bible:

> 'How are we to understand that God, the all-knowing, said to Adam "Where art thou"?'
>
> 'Do you believe,' answered the rav, 'that the Scriptures are eternal and that every era, every generation and every man is included in them?'
>
> 'I believe this,' said the other.
>
> 'Well then,' said the zaddik,[36] 'in every era, God calls to every man: "Where are you in your world? So many years and days of those allotted to you have passed, and how far have you got in your world?" God says something like this: "You have lived forty-six years. How far along are you?"'
>
> When the chief of the gendarmes heard his age mentioned, he pulled himself together, laid his hand on the rav's shoulder, and cried: 'Bravo!' But his heart trembled.

The tale seems so simple that a sophisticated modern reader might be tempted to dismiss it with a smile. But Buber points out some of the main implications. The reply is given on a different plane from that on which the question is asked. What was intended as generalized controversy receives a personal reply, and one which makes the questioner aware that he is concealing from himself the question that matters most to him: what he is doing with his life. We may press this a little farther. It is the gendarme and not the rabbi who now discovers himself to be a prisoner awaiting trial. The detective must investigate himself. The rabbi's answer 'illuminates both the situation of the biblical Adam and that of every man in every time and in every place'. God asks the question not that He may know but that Adam may be moved to answer it truthfully.

> Everything now depends on whether man faces the question. Of course, every man's heart, like that of the chief in the story, will tremble when he hears it. But his system of hide-outs will help him to overcome this emotion. For the

Voice does not come in a thunderstorm which threatens man's very existence; it is a 'still small voice', and easy to drown. So long as this is done, man's life will not become a *way*. Whatever success and enjoyment he may achieve, whatever power he may attain and whatever deeds he may do, his life will remain way-less, so long as he does not face the Voice. Adam faces the Voice, perceives his enmeshment, and avows: 'I hid myself'; this is the beginning of man's way. The decisive heart-searching is the beginning of the way in man's life; it is, again and again, the beginning of a human way.[37]

But Buber also warns against a sterile kind of heart-searching which leads to nothing but self-torture. There is a demonic, a spurious question, which follows 'Where art thou?' with 'From where you have got to, there is no way out'—acceptance of which appears to leave man no way of living but by demonic pride.

For the moment, this single example may serve. But it shows, as we shall find again and again as our enquiry develops, how the essential Hasidic teacher, in another land and in a very different century and cultural climate, appeals directly, naturally and spontaneously to Biblical myth, without any intervening doctrinal or ideological distortion or sophistication: how such a teacher finds, as Martin Buber finds in the Bible, in Hasidism and in his own twentieth century, the same archetypal pattern of the Wanderer, who is Everyman and whose inescapable name is Adam, and of the Way that begins only when he turns to the Voice that questions him, and of which there will be more to say in later chapters.

*   *   *

The real element of the marvellous in the Hasidic tale just quoted is that—without any breach in the 'natural' order of things or any untoward 'experience'—the dialogue between man and man turns into—is recognized as—a dialogue between man and God. Perhaps we may say that it was the latent 'rabbinical conscience' hidden by the police chief from himself, that led him to bring up—by way of argument and examination of his prisoner, as he supposed—the very question that the Rabbi's simple reply leads him to experience as really spoken by another voice, and really spoken to himself. The slight shock produced by the answer of the rabbinical voice is a shock of recognition, not disarray before a good debating point.

This is an archetype of what can and should occur in the experience of reality—not only of exchanges between man and man—by any man anywhere at any time. And the simplest and truest way of expressing this is to give man his right name:[38] 'in all the multiplicity and complexity', writes Buber of modern man, 'he has remained Adam. Now as always a real decision is made in him whether he faces the speech of God articulated to him in things and events—or escapes.'[39] These words, from a collection of works 'filling out and applying' what was said in *I and Thou* are sufficiently clear and precise to anyone who reads somewhat as Buber himself does—and few people do nowadays—giving full weight to every word. But perhaps their full implication is more apparent when we trace, as this chapter has endeavoured to do, the way that leads from interpretation of the first Book of the Hebrew Bible, through a moment of Hasidic illumination in which a spark is struck to life and which depends on the same Biblical source, and so on into the contemporary context in which man's identity with Adam is affirmed against all competing claims of modern ideologies and philosophies, the mistaken myths of our time. Man, Buber is saying, is incomprehensible—and in a certain sense virtually non-existent—unless realized as creature, addressed by his Creator through the creation. It is all and everything in this creation that is the true Torah, the Bible is the primer that teaches us how to read in it. As in the Bible, there is a limitless perspective through which we are addressed: the right response opens our way unpredictably before us from moment to moment.

Man faces the speech of God—or escapes. But the escape is not the escape of the whole man in some direction that he chooses or to which he is, as he feels, compelled. It is wandering, into self-division and beyond that to final nothingness. Buber has traced some of the more significant wanderings of the modern Adam as exemplified and made articulate by various representative spiritual and intellectual leaders.[40]

The rise of Hasidism coincided with the life of Immanuel Kant. Buber declares that what the great philospher ultimately sought and tried to apprehend as the cornerstone of his whole philosophy was, as he formulated the proposition in his old age, that 'God is not an external substance, but only a moral condition within us'.[41] And to avoid the disastrous objection that in this case each man might perhaps find within himself a different categorical imperative, Kant made not the individual but human society the arbiter: *vox dei, vox populi*. But to this human subjectivization or socialization of divinity Buber brings the conclusive witness of one's own deepest experience. Can one indeed always identify the social will with the absolute good and say, for instance, 'my country' without meaning also 'my country right *or wrong*'? But even more, can one always identify one's own dominant subjective impulse with absolute goodness? The conclusion that Buber finds inescapable is that 'the encounter with the original voice, the original source of yes or no, cannot be replaced by any self-encounter'.[42]

It is a short, and one might suppose inevitable, step from the proposition that God is only a moral condition within us to dispensing with the God-proposition altogether. In the nineteenth century Nietzsche did so with his famous proclamation that 'God is dead'. Nietzsche saw the self-led man not in terms of one dedicated, like Kant's man of good will, to equality and fraternity, but one gloriously given over to his individual will to power over the supine many.[43] This was the remorseless logic of the cult of the autonomous individual.

Religious individualism took an equally radical turn in Kierkegaard, for whom a man might not, upon his soul, have intimate relation with any other human being whatsoever. He clung desperately to the Adam who existed before all others of his kind and held converse with God alone.

In our time, Sartre combines the radical distrust of his fellow creatures that was common to Nietzsche and Kierkegaard with the emphatic atheism of the former. He denies the existence of God and, in two famous aphorisms, declares that 'Hell is other people' and 'Freedom is terror'. Even when a man makes common cause with the people, communication is impossible and he is finally alone. This godless and eternally solitary Adam is memorably dramatized in Sartre's play *Le Diable et Le Bon Dieu*, of which the protagonist is Goethe's Ironhand, Goetz.

But if 'God is dead' and Man is alienated from his world and his kind, can he, should he, exist at all? The dialogue that was threatened at one pole by Nietzsche's declaration was attacked at the other in our time—and in the name of Christian mysticism —by Simone Weil. Buber quotes her saying[44] 'We possess nothing in this world other than the power to say I. This is what we should yield up to God, and that is what we should destroy.'

Western culture has become a Babel of conflicting claims, but if there is any main tendency to be traced through it, Kant, Nietzsche, Kierkegaard, Sartre and Weil are not far away from it. The process seems plain, or becomes apparent in Buber's deeply understanding and dissenting scrutiny of it. First there comes denial of the dialogue between God and man, which is replaced by soliloquy or the social sanction. Then the denial of the now superfluous deity, who was a fiction of former and less enlightened times, now outgrown. Then, somewhat strangely but inevitably, the breakdown and denial of the possibility of true dialogue between man and man. Finally the casting away of the now isolated human person. What, other than Buber's teaching of *I and Thou*, the bond between Jonathan and David, the modern formulation from the very root of language of the traditional teaching of the dialogue between God and Adam, stands against this erosion into chaos and nothingness?

Many will answer that Kant's socialization of the source of right and wrong stands against it, and stands successfully as the reality that will endure. Let the age of individualism fade, the brighter era of socialism is dawning, an age in which the individual will be content to find his place and his meaning in the society of which he is no more than an economic cell. These basic assumptions, though not the full practice, of totalitarianism are now widely and deeply spread through the Western world. How often are all personal problems reduced to the need to 'adjust to society'—without any question of how the health and sanity of the society is to be evaluated, so long as it discharges more or less tolerably the distribution of goods and opportunity and does not lag behind others in technological development. In this chapter we are concerned with the individual Adam. It is true that he becomes the 'I' of the I–Thou relationship only in saying 'Thou' to his 'neighbours', to all and any of his fellow-creatures he actually encounters. But if he merely submerges or resigns his 'I' to the collective, the vital and basic dialogic relationship is again desecrated, the same process of disintegration sets in, the utopia of all for none. But we reserve Buber's critique of collectivism for the next chapter.

Buber does not, of course, believe that there can be any nostalgic turning back to a lost age of faith. Even this brief glance at his assessment of the plight of modern man and society adds weight to the words of his we quoted in the Introduction: 'The man of today has no access to a sure and solid faith, nor can it be made accessible to him. If he examines himself seriously, he knows this and may not delude himself further.'

What then? At the end of 1951, Martin Buber addressed a Jewish audience in New York. He pointed out that the command, 'Love thy neighbour as thyself' did not end there; it went on, 'I am the Lord'. 'And here,' he said, 'the Hasidic interpretation comes in: "You think I am far away from you, but in your love for your neighbour you will find me; not in his love for you but in yours for him."'

> He who loves brings God and the world together. The Hasidic teaching is the consummation of Judaism. And this is its message to all: *You yourself must begin.* Existence will remain meaningless for you if you yourself do not penetrate into it with active love and if you do not in this way discover its meaning for yourself. Everything is waiting to be hallowed by you; it is waiting to be disclosed in its meaning and to be realized in it by you. For the sake of this your beginning, God created the world. He has drawn it out of himself so that you may bring it closer to Him. Meet the world with the fullness of your being and you shall meet Him.[45]

When Buber went to Jerusalem from Germany early in 1938, his inaugural lectures in 'philosophical anthropology' were addressed to the question in which the pure reason of Kant is pierced by the despairing cry of Job—'What is Man?' He began with words once addressed by one of the last great teachers of Hasidism to his pupils: 'I wanted to write a book called *Adam*, which would be about the whole man. But then I decided not to write it.'[46] The story of the whole man cannot be written. Adam's answer to the divine question is still 'I hid myself'. And now he does not even answer because he no longer begins, 'I heard Thy voice in the garden . . .' When the whole man answers with his whole being Adam will have reached that culmination of history where he will no longer bear the same name as the dust itself. His name then will be Messiah.

2

THE WANDERING PEOPLE: NOAH

IN Martin Buber's directly Biblical writings there are three
treatments of the second great myth in the Book of Genesis.
Naturally they are very much alike. They are to be found—in
order of writing—in *The Prophetic Faith*,[1] *Images of Good and Evil*,[2]
and the vital article on 'Abraham the Seer'.[3] In the first of these
we read:

> . . . how YHVH Himself and no other was responsible for
> the nation's plurality. He had purposed a unity for mankind,
> but since the first mankind sinned and was punished for the
> deeds of violence which filled the earth (6:11), He set up a
> second mankind.

On a first reading one feels some initial surprise that even this
brief summary makes no allusion to the Flood, the Ark and
Noah, the human link between the first mankind and the second.

In the second account, the sense of strangeness persists.
Images of Good and Evil, we have already noted, makes a basic
distinction between two stages of evil, more or less corresponding
to inadvertent sin and deliberate wickedness, to drifting or
wandering on the one hand or denying or setting oneself against
the divine reality on the other. It is, at any rate, a clear distinction, though we are warned that the frontier is not plainly
marked, and one may pass from the first stage to the second like
a ship crossing the line on a starless night. The archetype of the
first condition is found in the myth of Adam, and Cain. In this
small book, the image of the second is found—in the Avesta.
Again one is perplexed. True, we are told that:

> This, however, in no way implies that in the Old Testament
> the first of these two conceptions was dominant. The story
> of the revolt of the race of men which sprang up again after
> the Flood, who built themselves a tower . . .[4]

—that this Biblical myth, in which we again hear nothing of the
presence of Noah, fully evoked the second stage of evil. Why,

then, the reader at first wonders, does Buber not use that myth
instead of the Avestic one, as his principal illustration of the
second phase?

Part of the answer, and an important one, is soon forthcoming.
The paragraph from which we have just quoted ends: 'The two
fundamental types of evil from indecision and evil from decision
are, therefore, not to be understood as having an ethnic basis.'
The significance of this statement may be underlined. We began
by establishing the primacy of myth in Buber's understanding of
religion. We emphasized his contention that the reality from
which myth sprang was to be sought in the depths of one's own
life-experience, where also we could alone find the criterion for
distinguishing true myth from false. But how are we to know
that, even in such scrupulous self-examination, we are not too
much influenced by being born into a particular civilization, a
specific religious and cultural tradition? The independent
testimony of another religion and people gives us as much
verification as we can expect to find that this is not so, that we
meet 'the thing itself, unaccommodated man'.[5]

But though this is true and valuable it is surely not the whole
explanation of Buber's illustrating the first stage of evil from the
Hebrew tradition and the second from the Iranian. He writes, as
always, as a Jew whom nothing can separate from the sacred
history of Israel. That the Jews stand accused and convicted,
in their Bible, of almost every imaginable sin is one of the things
that makes the book, so far as it is a nation's history, stand apart
from and above the histories written by any other nation about
itself. But, when all is said, this is within the extreme limit of
Buber's first stage of evil. Deliberately deny the one God or turn
their faces against Him the Jews did not. If any individual among
them does so, he ceases to be a Jew, not so much because of any
penalty his people might impose upon him, but by *de facto* self-
separation from them. After speaking of self-knowledge as the
way of verification of the myth of 'wandering' Buber concludes,
not quite impenetrably, 'Insight into the second stage, to which
the Ancient Iranian tales are to be related, must naturally be
gained along a different path'.[6] If one may say so, Martin Buber
lacked the ultimate qualification for writing about the second
stage of evil. Which is not to say that, having suffered the effects
of it in person and as an integral part of his afflicted people, he

lacks material or the ability to penetrate it as far as that may be done by anyone who does not 'know' it in himself.

We pass to the third of Buber's expositions of the second myth of Genesis.

> The first race of mankind, thus launched into the world and into the world's history, fails. But not because of the sin against God. The sin against God led only to the expulsion from Paradise. It is the sin of men against each other, the way of strife, beginning with fratricide and ending by filling the world with 'violence'; it is the wickedness of men that 'corrupts' the earth itself, which leads to the deluge. Once more the waters rise above the earth, as in the beginning. Preserved from those waters, the second generation of men is set upon the earth.[1]

And here, once more, no mention of Noah.

But this third treatment is mainly concerned with Abraham (and we shall depend largely upon it in the next chapter). In the section of it which follows that in which we read the passage just quoted, we find: 'Abraham must be related only to this second beginning because it alone, like the third, is based upon election. The juxtaposition is accomplished by comparing Abraham with that other chosen man, Noah.'[8] Now there follows a sufficient treatment of Noah himself, in which the reason for this long deferred appearance is made plain and vindicated. We cannot discern the limitations of the good natural father until we compare him with the chosen good father of the holy nation:

> Noah stands in his place in nature, as one who has been saved from the deluge, a 'husband-man'; Abraham is the first to make his way into history, a proclaimer of God's dominion.[9]

* * *

'It is the sin of men against each other, the way of strife, beginning with fratricide and ending by filling the world with "violence"; it is the wickedness of men that "corrupts" the earth itself, which leads to the deluge.' The evil between man and man (if it does not stem from *deliberate* repudiation of the sovereignty of God) is still 'wandering', it is within the farthest limits of the first stage of evil—though it is enough to doom 'the first race of mankind'.

Revolt against the kingship of God (even if it does not issue in fratricide but rather in a false solidarity) is the second and ultimate stage of evil. It threatens modern man as it did the builders of the Tower of Babel, with inner and outer annihilation.

Myth is above concept because it is the response of the whole man to his total experience. 'Everything conceptual in this connection is merely an aid, a useful bridge between myth and reality. Its construction is indispensable.'[10] Myth has its own superior way of expressing what intellectual analysis is searching for, it speaks simply in terms of the continuity of life itself.

Thus, if we enquire what were the further consequences of Adam's disobedience—beyond expulsion from a Paradisal harmony with nature into an 'indifferent' world—we have only to turn into thought the stories of the three sons that were born to him. Abel: that in Adam which was 'a keeper of sheep'[11] and for whose offering of the firstlings the Lord had respect. Cain: that in Adam which was firstborn and which destroyed Abel and became the guilt-striken wanderer. Seth: that in Adam which could, through his descendant Noah, survive the Flood—though only because 'Noah found grace in the eyes of the Lord'[12]—and preserve a human line, still not made whole, but in which might arise—again by divine election—the father of the third mankind, whose nation was destined to restore the primal wholeness of Man, to reunite 'Adam' through Messiah, in whom the Abel-element that perished long ago would reign supreme. Ultimately not only the sins but the goodness of the fathers will be visited upon the children.

Meanwhile, the Cain element threatens to over-run the whole development. The seed of Cain multiplies. By the seventh generation it has distorted God's warning of the self-perpetuating evil of blood-feud into a threat multiplied eleven times:

> If Cain shall be avenged sevenfold,
> Truly Lamech seventy and sevenfold.[13]

Only now do we read of Adam's fathering of a third son 'instead of Abel' and 'in his own likeness'.[14] From Seth spring more generations than are recorded of Cain, but the seed of Cain has destructive impulse enough to offset natural fruitfulness. 'The earth is filled with violence through them,'[15] God says to Noah. And it is clear from the way in which Noah's three sons, paralleling the first three sons, of Adam, are respectively cursed and blessed by their own father, that the elements of Cain and Seth have mingled. The first race of men escapes total annihilation—and the world of nature with them—only by becoming the second, only because Adam's third-born is ancestor to Noah's first-born, Shem—and the Lord is the God of Shem.[16]

Once, with Buber's direction, we have begun to take notice of 'dialogue' as the basic element in the Hebrew Bible, what is not there speaks as eloquently as what is. Adam talked with God—and wandered. God speaks to Noah and Noah does his bidding—but he does not speak in reply. Nor does he speak to man, as the prophets of Israel were to do, in warning and exhortation to the turning. Noah speaks only once, and the narrative then passes on in the next verse to describe his death a long time later. He curses his youngest son, the element of himself that will turn to worship false gods, to the practice of abomination and to occupation of the land intended for the seed of Shem, the eldest. He prays that God will enlarge Japheth, his second son, who shall dwell in the tents of Shem—the part of his own nature that is redeemable and will form the nations. And between that curse and that prayer he blesses the Lord, the God of Shem.[17] This threefold Noachic potentiality is what survives the threat of internecine slaughter in the man who heeds the negative commandment:

> Whoso sheddeth man's blood, by man shall his blood be shed; for in the image of God made He man.[18]

Once more, we are to remember that a man wrote this myth, out of his total encounter with divine reality. It is true of the second man. He loves peace. His firstborn is Shem.

*　　*　　*

At the roots of language there are words that express opposite meanings. One such, whose duality still flourishes in modern English usage, is the verb 'to cleave'. We cleave together. We cleave asunder. What the second race of man has to learn is that there is a way of cleaving together that *is* a way of cleaving asunder:

> And now the second race of man also fails; this time, by sinning against God. The strangest thing about this sin is that it is the outcome of an intention the precise opposite of

that which constituted the first sin. The first race of men instead of clinging together had divided man from man, beginning with the murder of brother by brother. The second race of men wants to join together—in the wrong way. The first had missed its aim to become an undivided humanity by an act of violence; the second wants to remain together in its city to avoid dispersal, to work together, to be united in a common humanity—by rising up against God. The shared work centres in the tower, its spire pointing to heaven, against heaven . . .

But now, as punishment for the perverse kind of unity, comes the dispersal. In answer to their 'lest we be scattered' comes the reiterated 'scattered them' which reports God's action . . . The humanity which was none because it sought union *against* God is 'scattered' into nations; the one earth is broken up into countries, and the one language ('lip') into languages ('tongues'). The most explicit symbol of the new situation is that now no one understands the other. And in the midst of the transformed human world, the world of nations, there stands the unfinished, unfinishable city, Babel, city of 'confusion'. Such is the state of the humanity into which Abram is born . . .[19]

The physical scattering through the world in rival and hostile nations, the multiplicity of languages, these are the ways in which myth speaks and history speaks, in which myth is history and history is myth, of the breakdown of the dialogue between man and man that follows inexorably upon the denial of the true dialogue between man and God.

*   *   *

We pass to Hasidism. It is a transition from the violent first race of men who almost destroyed mankind forever and the gregarious second race of men, sundered in their self-sufficient ant-hill, as evoked in the Biblical myths of pre-history, to an eighteenth-century C.E. Europe where the difficulty lies in finding any fundamental difference in the human condition. Noachic man is fighting with his back to the wall to sustain himself against the sons of Cain—it is often difficult to know which is which—who are threatening a come-back and, indeed, have not left the scene since the dawn of history. As to the third race of men, as the descendants of Abraham are called, it is not easy to find them at all, scattered as they too are among the warring nations. It would seem to most historians the height of eccentricity or fanaticism to see the Hasidim, if they have been heard of at all above the hubbub of 'history', as a phenomenon of any but the most local and transient significance.

To understand the background against which Hasidism appeared, we need a lightning sketch of the scene. We can on the whole do no better than borrow from an Englishman who, in our time, put the history of the world and of mankind into a single volume. If there was a typical Noachic man in England in the first half of the twentieth century, few have better claim to the name than H. G. Wells. He may have thought so too. Towards the end of his life, after World War II had begun, he put out a small book entitled *All Aboard for Ararat*. As the 'All' of that title might imply, Wells—not like Noah a silent man—also aspired to the status of prophet. *God the Invisible King* (1917) had preceded *The Outline of History* (1920) and that was followed in the next decade by *The Shape of Things to Come: the ultimate revolution* (1933). The nations were to abandon their selfishness and their bellicosity and—pushed and led by disaster and science respectively—to merge their petty identities in the World State. Wells believed that this would happen. The title and date of his last book, *Mind at the End of its Tether* (1945) reveal the bitterness of his disillusion and the terrible occasion of it. His Ark of Reason had foundered. His friends hastened to say that he was dying at the time. But perhaps, in his final despair of the possibility of building the universal world community on the basis of biological intelligence alone, at the last he came near to the note that had been heard from the prophets of old, and which also had not been favourably received.

The Outline of History, whatever shortcomings specialists and others may detect in it, remains an important book, not least for its admirably plain speaking, and because the pace at which the narrative unfolds at last gives us glimpses of the over-all picture. Wells was no friend to Great Powers or to Priests, and Jews and Judaism come in for fairly rough but thoroughly honest and well-meant evaluation. Early in the chapter on 'The Hebrew Scriptures and their Prophets' Wells summed up the strategic situation:

> The position of the land of Judea and of Jerusalem, its
> capital, is a peculiar one . . . through it lies the natural
> high road between the Hittites, Syria, Assyria and Babylonia
> to the north and Egypt to the south. It was a country pre-
> destined, therefore, to a stormy history. Across it Egypt, and
> whatever power was ascendant in the north, fought for
> empire . . .

And later in the chapter:

> So the four centuries of Hebrew kingship came to an end.
> From first to last it was a mere incident in the larger and
> greater history of Egypt, Syria, Assyria and Phoenicia. But
> out of it there were now to arise moral and intellectual con-
> sequences of primary importance to all mankind.[20]

Unlike the Hebrew kings, the prophets come in for favour-
able mention. In their way they were really as promising as
Herodotus.[21]

We turn over some five hundred and fifty pages, to the section
on 'The Growth of the Idea of Great Powers'. Assyria and Egypt
are gone. So too are Greece and Rome, as Great Powers anyway.
The section begins:

> We have seen how the idea of a world-rule and a community
> of mankind first came into human affairs, and we have
> traced how the failure of the Christian churches to sustain
> and establish those conceptions of its founder, led to a moral
> collapse in political affairs, and a reversion to egotism and
> want of faith. We have seen how Machiavellian monarchy
> set itself up against the spirit of brotherhood in Christendom
> and how Machiavellian monarchy developed throughout a
> large part of Europe into the Grand Monarchies and
> Parliamentary Monarchies of the seventeenth and eigh-
> teenth centuries.[22]

The next section, significantly perhaps, focuses on 'The
Crowned Republic of Poland and its Fate' as the epitome of the
process of history at that time. We read that 'the mass of her
population was a downtrodden and savagely ignorant peasantry,
and she also harboured great masses of very poor Jews'.[23] We
turn the page and, at one opening, are faced with four maps,
showing the Poland of the last quarter of the eighteenth century.

Russia and Austria crush it like iron jaws, it shrinks and, with some help from Prussia and the Ottoman Empire, disappears from the map. We have seen the process repeated, a precarious Poland divided between a totalitarian Germany and a totalitarian Russia, in our time. Geographically and historically, the parallel to the little land of Palestine, caught between Assyria and Egypt, is striking.

The Poland of the four maps in *The Outline of History* is the Poland of Hasidism. The founder of Hasidism, the Baal Shem Tov, had died about 1760. The movement he had founded continued to grow and spread for another hundred years. Martin Buber was born in Vienna in 1878 and lived until he was fourteen 'in the Galician home of his grandfather, Solomon Buber, a distinguished scholar. There he received a thorough Jewish education in the traditional style, and first came into contact with Hasidism, which was to become one of the great formative influences of his life and thought.'[24] When, in 1928, he spoke of 'The Faith of Judaism'[25] he said, at the beginning:

> In Hasidism I see merely a concentrated movement, the concentration of all those elements which are to be found in a less condensed form everywhere in Judaism, even in 'rabbinic' Judaism. Only, in rabbinic Judaism this movement is not visible in the structure of the community, but holds sway over the inaccessible structure of the personal life.

Much earlier he had simply said,[26] 'No renewal of Judaism is possible that does not bear in itself the elements of Hasidism.' What happened in the middle of the eighteenth century in this 'European Palestine' which was soon to vanish from the map was a new concentration of the scattered Judaism, which became visible in the structure of new Jewish communities. With that we shall be concerned later.

*   *   *

... in his twenty-sixth year, 1904, he happened to read a statement of Rabbi Israel ben Eliezer (1700–1760) the so named *Baal Shem Tov*, founder of the Hasidic movement, in which the Baal Shem describes the intensity and depth of the daily renewal expected of each Hasid. In this description Buber recognized within himself precisely this quality of intensity and return. As a result of this experience and its consequences, Buber retired from his journalistic and Zionist activities and engaged for a period of five years in close study of Hasidic texts.[27]

The first volume of the *Tales of the Hasidism* has the statement: 'This book contains less than a tenth of the material I collected.'[28] Buber was well aware that, apart from the excesses of the decline that set in about a century after the death of the Baal Shem, the Hasidim were not seldom given to pious exaggeration. A most useful but less discerning Hasidic anthology[29] gives, for instance, this:

> As the first of the Hasidim appears Adam (Erubin 18b), but as the first of the Zaddikim, Noah, of whom Holy Writ gives this account: 'He was a Zaddik entire in his generation, and he walked with God.' (Genesis 6:9.)

Buber, in an article not directly connected with Hasidism,[30] writes:

> Noah is the first person in Scripture to whom epithets are attached. He is said to have been 'righteous' (*zaddik*) and 'whole' (*tamin*) in 'his generations', i.e. in the generations encompassed by his life span . . .
>   The three words 'righteousness', 'wholeness', and 'walking with God' turn up again in the story of Abraham, and just as Noah is characterized only by those three, no others are joined to them in the description of Abraham. But here they reappear in a strangely altered way . . .

We shall be concerned with the superiority of Abraham in the next chapter. Here we need only point out that the difference is that between the father of the 'second mankind' and that of the 'third mankind'. The zaddik-ship of Noah is, to say the least, an honorary degree. The true zaddik did not produce a community in which, as in the second race of man, there was a complete breakdown of communication. And, as the true hasid was, if nothing else, loyally devoted to his zaddik it is perhaps as well to follow Buber's example and enquire no farther into the hasidship of Adam.

    In history there is no going back, however much there may be back-sliding. The problem of the true zaddik was how to overcome the barrier between man and man that had been set up by the 'confusion of tongues', a barrier that was towering not only between the hostile Great Powers of his time but had invaded the holy nation at least sufficiently to cause conflict between orthodox rabbinic scholars and the unpredictable Hasidim. In the following story from the first volume of *Tales of the Hasidim*, there is no direct reference to Babel, but the allusion is plain enough. Seventy, of course, was the traditional number of nations into which the second mankind was divided:

Rabbi Leib, son of Sarah, the hidden zaddik, told:

'Once I was with the Baal Shem Tov over the sabbath. Toward evening, his great disciples gathered around the table before the third meal and waited for his coming. And while waiting, they discussed a passage in the Talmud about which they wanted to ask him. It was this: "Gabriel came and taught Joseph seventy languages." They could not understand this, for does not every language consist of countless words? Then, how could the mind of one man grasp them all in a single night, as the passage implied? The disciples decided that Rabbi Gershon of Kitov, the Baal Shem's brother-in-law, should be the one to ask him.

'When he came and seated himself at the head of the table, Rabbi Gershon put the question. The Baal Shem began to say words of teaching, but what he said seemed to have nothing to do with the subject of the question, and his disciples could not glean an answer from his words. But suddenly something unheard-of and incredible happened. In the middle of the Baal Shem's address, Rabbi Jacob Joseph rapped on the table and called out: "Turkish!" and after a while: "Tartar!" and after another interval: "Greek!" and so on, one language after another. Gradually his companions understood; from the master's speech, which was apparently concerned with quite different things, he had come to know the source and the character of every single language—and he who teaches you the source and character of a language, has taught you the language itself.'[31]

To this sufficiently transparent tale of the Baal Shem Tov, the true zaddik who speaks with his whole self turned to God, thus drawing on the source of meaning upon which all languages depend, must be added part of another. This depends on the belief that whatever befalls man also befalls Nature, or his experience of Nature's twofoldness. The second race of man not only fails to communicate with his fellow man, he fails also to understand the 'speech' of nature, he is an alien in a world that speaks an unknown tongue and which he may suspect to speak nothing that has any value; that is to say, it does not proclaim its divine source.[32]

> Rabbi Arye, the preacher of Polnay, nourished a burning desire for a wisdom that is so rare among mortals that in each age only one single individual is its heir and guardian. In the days when Rabbi Arye walked the earth and struggled for its possession, it was the Baal Shem who was the master of it.
>
> The bearer of this wisdom could understand the language of all creatures. He perceived what the animals on the earth and in the air confided to one another about the secrets of their existence; indeed, even what the trees and plants spoke to one another was known to him. If he laid his ear to the black earth or to the bare rock, the whispering of the creatures who shun the light and dwell in crevices and caves reached him.

Here we can give only this beginning and the end of the extensive tale, as Buber relates it in one of the works of his early five year withdrawal from public affairs to study Hasidism. Rabbi Arye approaches the Baal Shem and eventually is invited to sit beside him in his carriage as they drive into the country. The Baal Shem knows the Rabbi's wish without being told. When he comes to reveal the heart of the secret he commands,

> Therefore, bend your ear close to my mouth and listen to me with your whole soul. Shut yourself off in this moment from all that exists, outside of you and my words!

But as he listens, the Rabbi hears also the morning song of the birds—and understands it!

> The forest cleared, and already they could see before them the city which was the goal of their journey. The Baal Shem had now finished his instruction and glanced inquiringly at

the preacher. 'Have you mastered well what you have learned from me?' he asked after awhile.

Rabbi Arye looked at him radiantly with self-assured eyes. 'Yes, Master,' he replied. 'I have understood everything well!'

Then the Baal Shem passed the palm of his hand lightly over his forehead.

Now the rabbi forgot all, all that the Baal Shem had revealed to his spirit. He sat there, inconsolably empty and as if burnt out, listened to the birds chirping in the furrows and understood of it as little as he ever had before this day— it was nothing but an animal's simple, senseless sound!

But the Baal Shem smiled and said, 'Alas for you, Rabbi Arye, you have a greedy soul! Could you not devote your soul to me entirely in the moment when I wished to instil the knowledge into it? Alas for you, friend, you wanted to enrich yourself immoderately and in haste! God's wonders are for those who can collect themselves in one thing and be satisfied in it.'

Sobbing, the preacher hid his face in his hands.

The wholeness of Adam divided three ways in his sons, or rather two, since Seth was given to him 'instead of Abel'. The wholeness of the righteous Noah was divided three ways, one of which, the first-born, was the way of Shem, the ancestor of Abram. The new wholeness to which the third race of men is directed has not yet grown from this seed to full stature. Insofar as it comes into existence in the all-exclusive, all-inclusive dialogue between man and man, the way through the world lies open, and the city that now rises into sight is a recognizable Jerusalem.

> The primary word I–Thou can only be spoken with the whole being.[33]
> Every particular Thou is a glimpse through to the eternal Thou . . .[34]

* * *

In the last third of the first chapter we caught glimpses of how the positions of a few representative modern religious and non-religious philosophers appear in the perspective of the myth of

Adam and the disruption of his dialogue with God. Now, since
we are mainly concerned with larger human groups and indeed
with the entire human family, we turn to the main trends of
modern political and sociological thought, as manifested in the
actual conduct of large human societies. After what has been
said already about the fatal division of the race of Cain that lapses
into fratricidal violence, and the more evil, because ultimately
more fatal, false cohesion of the self-sufficient, sky-aspiring men
of Babel who no longer understand each other, little more will be
necessary in the way of comment on a few passages from Buber's
writings on modern manifestations of these phenomena. Of
man's relation to nature we can scarcely speak at all. As far as
modern man is concerned it is there to be enjoyed and exploited
and that is the end of the matter.

After his retirement from his chair at the Hebrew University
of Jerusalem in 1951, Martin Buber undertook a lecture tour in
the United States. At the end of the year he gave to a Jewish
audience, under the auspices of the Jewish Theological Seminary,
the Israel Goldstein Lectures for that year, three addresses—
'Judaism and Civilization', 'The Silent Question'[35] and 'The
Dialogue between Heaven and Earth'[36]—whose titles speak for
themselves, afterwards published as *At the Turning*,[37] a small book
which is now hard to find. At a parting celebration before a more
mixed American audience in the Carnegie Hall, New York, he
gave an address published[38] as 'Hope for this Hour':

> During the First World War it became clear to me that a
> process was going on which before then I had only surmised.
> This was the growing difficulty of genuine dialogue, and
> most especially of genuine dialogue between men of differ-
> ent kinds and convictions. Direct, frank dialogue is becom-
> ing ever more difficult and more rare; the abysses between
> man and man threaten ever more pitilessly to become un-
> bridgeable. I began to understand at that time, more than
> thirty years ago, that this is the central question for the fate
> of mankind. Since then I have continually pointed out that
> the future of man as man depends upon a rebirth of dia-
> logue.[39]

This was prefaced by a more direct reflection on the two camps
into which the post World War II world was dividing:

The human world is today, as never before, split into two camps, each of which understands the other as the embodiment of falsehood and itself as the embodiment of truth. Often in history, to be sure, national groups and religious associations have stood in so radical an opposition that the one side denied and condemned the other in its innermost existence. Now, however, it is the human population of our planet generally that is so divided, and with rare exceptions this division is everywhere seen as a necessity of existence in this world hour. He who makes himself an exception is suspected or ridiculed by both sides. Each side has assumed monopoly of the sunlight and has plunged its antagonist into night, and each side demands that you decide between day and night.

We can comprehend the origin of this cruel and grotesque condition in its simplest lines if we realize how the three principles of the French Revolution have broken asunder. The abstractions freedom and equality were held together there through the more concrete fraternity, for only if men feel themselves to be brothers can they partake of a genuine freedom from one another and a genuine equality with one another. But fraternity has been deprived of its original meaning, the relationship between children of God, and consequently of any real content. As a result, each of the two remaining watchwords was able to establish itself against the other and, by so doing, to wander farther and farther from its truth. Arrogant and presumptuous, each sucked into itself, ever more thoroughly, elements foreign to it, elements of passion for power and greed for possession.[40]

Later he characterized the breakdown of fraternity by reference to the two dominant influences in modern thought about freedom, on the one hand, and equality, on the other:

My main task in my intercourse with my fellow-man becomes more and more, whether in terms of individual psychology or of sociology, to see through and unmask him. In the classical case this in no wise means a mask he has put on to deceive me, but a mask that has, without his knowing it, been put on him, indeed positively imprinted on him, so that what is really deceived is his own consciousness. There are, of course, innumerable transitional forms.

With this changed basic attitude, which has found scientific rationalization in the teachings of Marx and Freud, the mistrust between man and man has become existential. This is so indeed in a double sense: It is, first of all, no longer only the uprightness, the honesty of the other, which is in question, but the inner integrity of his existence itself. Secondly, this mistrust not only destroys trustworthy talk between opponents, but also the immediacy of togetherness of man and man generally. Seeing-through and unmasking is now becoming the great sport between men, and those who practise it do not know whither it entices them. Nietzsche knew what he was doing when he praised the 'art of mistrust', and yet he did not know. For this game naturally only becomes complete as it becomes reciprocal, in the same measure as the unmasker himself becomes the object of unmasking. Hence one may foresee in the future a degree of reciprocity in existential mistrust where speech will turn into dumbness and sense into madness.[41]

And the conclusion is already in sight:

The hope for this hour depends upon the renewal of dialogical immediacy between men. But let us look beyond the pressing need, the anxiety and care of this hour. Let us see this need in connection with the great human way. Then we shall recognize that immediacy is injured not only between man and man, but also between the being called man and the source of his existence. At its core the conflict between mistrust and trust of man conceals the conflict between mistrust and trust of eternity. If our mouths succeed in genuinely saying 'thou', then, after long silence and stammering, we shall have addressed our eternal 'Thou' anew. Reconciliation leads towards reconciliation.[42]

*　　*　　*

In 1945 he had completed *Paths in Utopia*, in which he traced the Marxian abandonment of organic socialism for the centralized impersonal society. Here the separation of man from man in the closely knit modern industrial society was anatomized:

In the monstrous confusion of modern life, only thinly disguised by the reliable functioning of the economic and State-apparatus, the individual clings desperately to the collectivity. The little society in which he was embedded cannot help him; only the great collectivities, so he thinks, can do that, and he is all too willing to let himself be deprived of personal responsibility: he only wants to obey. And the most valuable of all goods—the life between man and man—gets lost in the process; the autonomous relationships become meaningless, personal relationships wither; and the very spirit of man hires itself out as a functionary. The personal human being ceases to be the living member of a social body and becomes a cog in the 'collective' machine. Just as his degenerate technology is causing man to lose the feel of good work and proportion, so the degrading social life he leads is causing him to lose the feel of community— just when he is so full of the illusion of living in perfect devotion to his community.[43]

And as we must banish the spectre of the first race of violent men that looms over the cold war and the atomic bomb, still more must we banish the demon that would make this Babel a global society of non-communicating units:

We must begin, obviously, with the establishment of a vital peace which will deprive the political principle of its supremacy over the social principle. And this primary objective cannot in its turn be reached by any devices of political organization, but only by the resolute will of all peoples to cultivate the territories and raw materials of our planet and govern its inhabitants, *together*. At this point, however, we are threatened by a danger greater than all the previous ones: the danger of a gigantic centralization of power covering the whole planet and devouring all free community. Everything depends on not handing the work of planetary management over to the political principle.[44]

Buber's meaning is plain for all to see. There will still be those who shake their heads regretfully and say that all this is a vain longing to reverse the irreversible course of history. Their God, it would seem, is not the God of history, but is being defeated by his own creation. This is not the religion of the Hebrew Bible, it is not Buber's. He had taken his stand soon after the First World War, in *I and Thou*:

> The quasi-biological and quasi-historical thought of to-day, however different the aims of each, have worked together to establish a more tenacious and oppressive belief in fate than has ever before existed.[45]

But this comment follows hard upon a very different diagnosis:

> The sickness of our age is like that of no other age, and it belongs together with them all. The history of cultures is not a course of aeons in which one runner after another has to traverse gaily and unsuspectingly the same death-track. A nameless way runs through their rise and fall: not a way of progress and development but a spiral descent through the spiritual underworld, which can also be called an ascent to the innermost, finest, most complicated whirlpool, where there is no advance and no retreat, but only utterly new reversal—the break through. Shall we have to go this way to the end, to trial of the final darkness? Where there is danger, the rescuing force grows too.[46]

3

THE WAYFARER: ABRAHAM

We have already quoted a decisive sentence from Martin Buber's comparison or contrast between Noah and Abraham:

> Noah stands in his place in nature, as one who has been saved from the deluge, a 'husband-man'; Abraham is the first to make his way into history, a proclaimer of God's dominion.

This does not mean that we are henceforward concerned only with 'facts' and not with 'myths'. It is precisely the twofold nature of the truth that is both essential fact and essential myth, the product of the 'shaping memory' that 'stands under a law'— and that 'law' the will of God—that constitutes the uniqueness of the Hebrew Bible:

> It is not that the biblical figures are unhistorical. I believe that we are standing at the beginning of a new era in biblical studies; whereas the past era was concerned with proving that the Bible did not contain history, the coming era will succeed in demonstrating its historicity. By this I do not mean that the Bible depicts men and women and events as they were in actual history; rather do I mean that its descriptions and narratives are the organic, legitimate ways of giving an account of what existed and what happened. I have nothing against calling these narratives myths and sagas, so long as we remember that myths and sagas are essentially memories which are actually conveyed from person to person. But what kind of memory is it which manifests itself in these accounts? I say again: memory; not imagination. It is an organic memory moulding its material . . .
> This being the case, we cannot disentangle the historical from the biblical. The power of the biblical writing, which springs from this shaping memory, is so great, the elemental

57

nature of this memory so mighty, that it is quite impossible to extract any so-called historical matter from the Bible. The historical matter thus obtained would be unreal, amorphous, without significance.[1]

But nor is it enough to suppose that the Bible 'just growed' without the fully conscious interaction of men of many different kinds in whom that organic memory flourished with greater or less power:

> One might object that no unified conception can be gained from the biblical story since it is known to have been put together from numerous fragments of various books, the so-called 'sources' coming out of different periods and determined by different tendencies. But even this theory, so dear to the eighteenth and nineteenth centuries, has been badly shaken. It appears that a book like the Book of Genesis could not have been put together like a cheap newspaper, with the help of scissors and paste. Many expressions and turns of phrase formerly thought to be characteristic of one or another 'source' increasingly reveal their meaning and their intent within a well-ordered whole.[2]

This is not an argument for single human authorship. Rather is it the written witness of the true community forming from diverse elements under the all-powered influence of a single source of inspiration:

> My ear, too, distinguishes a variety of voices in the chorus. Even the most ancient memories are likely to have been preserved from a variety of motives and will accordingly have been rendered in a variety of tones. Later chroniclers and scribes are even more likely to differ from one another in their treatment of the material and their style of representation: prophets differ naturally from court officials in their way of telling a story, as their motives differ, while a prophet with an official position at court will develop a different manner from that of an independent prophet, and a priest, insofar as priests took part in telling this story, is something else again.
>
> And yet this story has an amazingly homogeneous character, although the homogeneity did not exist from the beginning, but developed in time. For all the chroniclers, i.e. all the

custodians of the tradition, regardless of any particular tendencies or peculiarities of each individual, inhabit a common spiritual atmosphere which I would like to designate as proto-biblical, that is, the biblical atmosphere that existed before the Bible. All who contributed something to the history of beginnings—the beginning of the world, of the human race, of Israel—were ultimately concerned, each in his own way, with one thing; to show the people how their God prepared the goal and the road for them, even before they were yet a people.[3]

So Buber goes on to speak of the great men, whom he believes came no later than the final period of the Kingdom of Solomon, who went to work to express this unity in the multiplicity of the traditional stories of the Book of Genesis:

And now story is entwined with story, insofar as this had not yet been done, not infrequently by means of words rare in their context but recurring in the different narratives, and all fitted together in an almost symmetrically articulated architectonic structure, as is the story of Abraham. Only the realization of this tectonic unity the achievement of an image-making religious composing on a large scale, enables us to see in what way the Bible wants Abraham to be understood. . . . The Bible tells us its conception of Abraham; but at the core of this conception, there is something remembered.[4]

* * *

The story of the three races of mankind—turning into the dimension of history, as it where, the threefold emanations of Adam and Noah in their sons—is also the myth of the three dimensions of Man; or insofar as we can still say that the first race of men was destroyed, the seed of Cain is no more—the twofold Noachic–Abrahamic Man. Abrahamic dimension is what emerges—because it answers a call—from the Noachic, from the man who has renounced violence. The sign of that transfiguration is that the name Abram is expanded to Abraham. It is necessary to be explicit about this, at the risk of some offence, if we are truly to understand the Hebraism of Martin Buber and the ground on which he stands against another emphasis in

Judaism. Judaism is hardly dogmatic, but Maimonides' Thirteen Articles of the Faith are authoritative. The seventh— it is doubtless no accident that this is the central article of the thirteen—is: 'Belief in Moses as the greatest of the prophets.'[5] The Authorized Daily Prayer Book's wording of this is even more explicit:

> I believe with perfect faith that the prophecy of Moses our teacher, peace be unto him, was true, and that he was the chief of the prophets, both of *those that preceded* and of those that followed him.[6] (Our italics.)

It must at once be added that the preceding article has briefly proclaimed:

> I believe with perfect faith that all the words of the prophets are true.

To the present writer it appears that Buber would accept the latter formulation but would have some reservation as to the former. He does not award precedence, in that sense. The very title and whole trend of his great article 'Abraham the Seer' is to establish Abraham as the first prophet. His appreciation of Moses we shall consider briefly in the next chapter. But it was not for him, even if it was for Maimonides, to elevate the one above the other. Between Abraham and Moses, perhaps, he would allow no judge but God.

The role of the two prophets, however, was very different. Abraham was the solitary wayfarer who separated himself from society and kindred to found a new family, a new nation and ultimately a new humanity; he is the archetypal figure of the true relation between individual man and God. Moses was the prophetic man who bore the vast burden of ordering a human grouping traditionally estimated at 600,000 souls, newly emerged from slavery to Egypt. The first family had grown into twelve families, into twelve tribes, and the task of Moses was to show that potential community the way of transformation into the community of communities, into the new thing, the thirteenth entity, the holy nation. Who indeed shall judge between Abraham and Moses?

*   *   *

It is possible, or at least it is possible for the Bible, to judge between Abraham and Noah:

> The three words 'righteouness', 'wholeness', and 'walking with God' turn up again in the story of Abraham, and just as Noah is characterized only by those three, no others are joined to them in the description of Abraham. But here they reappear in a strangely altered way . . .[7]

Noah was said by Scripture to have been righteous (*zaddik*) which Buber interprets as:

> agreement between 'within' and 'without', between a 'truth' and a 'reality', between the rightness of a cause and its recognition, between conviction and behaviour.[8]

Noah, as we noted, does not speak, he acts, in actions that speak louder than many people's words. This he has in common with Abraham, except that Abraham, as we shall soon see, really speaks too in words that are more pregnant than most people's actions.

> Noah was also whole (*tamin*) which Buber interprets as: a harmony among the parts and qualities of a man, a unity of being, and a perfection of being.[9]

In the central one of the seven revelations to Abraham, his belief in the Lord is counted to him 'for righteousness':

> i.e. it is not said of Abraham as it was of Noah, that he was a righteous man; only a single characteristic or attitude of his makes him appear righteous in the eyes of God. (Genesis 15:6.)[10]

And the wholeness of Abraham is mentioned—

> not in the form of a statement, but in that of a command. God seems to command Abraham to become that which Noah was by nature! This does appear to reverse the order of rank of the two men.[11]
>
> Jewish tradition was on the right track when it found the solution to it in the words 'in his generations'. Noah, accordingly, was righteous and whole not in the absolute sense but only in relation to the corrupt or questionable generations of his time . . . Noah is truly one who is bound

up with his 'generations'—despite the fact that as a 'husband-man' (9:20) he renews agriculture and frees the soil from the curse. He has received no call which goes beyond this, against shedding blood, which is addressed to him (and) is meant for all; of him nothing is demanded that he, and he alone, must accomplish for future generations; nor does he, like Abraham, prefigure with his life the life of the people destined to become the model community for the nations of mankind.[12]

But the decisive difference between Noah and Abraham is expressed in the difference of wording of the third point on which the two may be compared. Noah 'walked with God'. Abraham receives the command 'walk before me!' To 'walk with God' is not a metaphor for a pious way of life pleasing to God. It is something like the negative virtue of not disobeying any commandment which is actually given. 'Walk before me!' is something far more active and adventurous, as well as being the higher honour:

> we see an image of the ruler at peace sending a herald ahead to announce his coming and prepare his way for a visit in person to a city in his realm. Precisely this is Abraham's office . . .
>
> As the herald of the Lord, Abraham goes before Him, the King of the future Israel, making his way throughout the province of the Lord which He will some day make His dwelling place, and proclaims it as God's property and residence by calling out His name.[13]

*   *   *

With Abraham what matters is not his character as God finds it, so to speak, but what he does, and what he becomes. His faith, which the Lord counts to him for righteousness, the fact that he trusts in God *before* God has fulfilled the promise, is thus significantly contrasted with the very different 'faith' of the people who trust in God only after Moses has given them signs (Exodus 4:31) . . .[14]

The first step of the long way is taken at the bidding of a nameless longing. It is only in the central revelation of the seven that Abraham understands:

Haran was not the first place out of which God's call brought Abram; God took him out of Ur, without Abram's realizing it, to bring him to the land.[15]

We cannot speak here of the sign of the covenant and the climax of dedication in which the whole living future is offered on the eminence of the land that is called Mount Moriah: YHWH Will See. Nor of the contention with God over Sodom, or the partings with Lot and with Ishmael that tell us something about certain elements in Abraham's nature 'as God finds it' and the necessary separation from them. We must here keep literally down to earth, to the land, which is claimed as the bridgehead for what will ultimately be the universal Kingdom.

The first three revelations to Abraham are progressively concerned with the land. First, God sends Abraham out of his house into the land which He will 'let him see'. Second, when he has come into the land God also 'lets him see' Himself. Abraham is the first man in Scripture to 'see' God. Third, after the separation from Lot, it is a matter of seeing the entire land, through which he will travel to take possession of it for his people.

> And in the third revelation it is (so) entirely a matter of land, of 'earth', that even 'the dust of the earth' necessarily becomes a metaphor for the increase of population; it is only in connection with this land that the people will be able to fulfil their task.[16]

This 'becoming' of the dust of the earth into the image of the population of which Abraham bears the seed, essentially repeats the formation from the *adamah* (earth) of the *adam* (man). It is the second creation of man, of man at last capable not only of wholeness but of holiness. Adam could hear and answer but did not do. Noah could hear and do but did not answer. Abraham could hear, answer and do. Dialogic man is Abrahamic man. He must stand his ground in the world, in harmony with it as Adam once was, husbanding it as Noah did, possessing it in God's name and for God's purpose:

> Three things in the Bible are traced back to Abraham. The first, overtly, is the origin of the people; the second, by connection with the people's past history, is the mission of the

people to become a community of nations; the third, by the indications of the story itself, is the birth of prophecy.[17]

* * *

Deliberate separation—the physical separation carries into deed the essential inner separation—from what is at best Noachic society and from what is Noachic in one's own family even, are preliminary to the encounter with God in the Abrahamic myth; and there is still the separation from Lot and Ishmael to be accomplished even after that. We may briefly notice here that an extreme 'separation' is implicit in the story of Isaac, the willing sacrifice in the next generation, who accepts death and yet does not die. Even so, yet another separation is required between his offspring, Esau and Jacob. The winnowing of the originally Noachic personality of Abraham is severe in the extreme, though a place is found in the world for Lot, Ishmael and Esau too. There is an inward as well as an outward separation from the 'second race' of man.

This element in the Hebrew tradition, springing as it does from the fountain-head, long before the people Israel is bidden to be a nation apart, is naturally expressed in the Hasidic revival which may be said to have been, on the whole, markedly more Abrahamic than Mosaic in character. Hence the antagonism of its rabbinic contemporaries, of some of whom it may perhaps be fairly said that the opposite was true.

For instance, among the 'Early Masters' of Hasidism, Rabbi Zusya emphasizes the inward separation which might not be obvious to the literal-minded reader of Genesis:

> God said to Abraham: 'Get thee out of thy country, and from thy kindred, and from thy father's house, unto the land that I will show thee.' God says to man: 'First, get you out of your country, that means the dimness you have inflicted on yourself. Then out of your birth-place, that means, out of the dimness your mother inflicted on you. After that, out of the house of your father, that means, out of the dimness your father inflicted on you. Only then will you be able to go to the land that I will show you.'[18]

Whereas, among the 'Later Masters'—by which time the Hasidic virtue of seeking God's presence in every element had begun to be confused with enjoying the good things of life in a rather different sense—Rabbi Abraham Yehoshua Heshel finds it pertinent to stress the outward dangers of religious individualism:

> The rabbi of Apt was asked: 'The Midrash points out that God said 'Go' twice to Abraham, once when he bade him leave his father's house, and once when he commanded him to sacrifice his son. The explanation in the Midrash is that the first bidding as well as the second was a test. How are we to understand that?'
>
> He replied: 'When God bade Abraham leave his father's house, he promised to make of him "a great nation". The Evil Urge observed with what eagerness he prepared himself for the journey and whispered to him: "You are doing the right thing. A great nation—that mean power, that means possessions!"'
>
> But Abraham only laughed at him. 'I understand better than you,' he said, '"A great nation"—means a people that sanctifies the name of God.'[19]

Both these stories, of course, are fairly simple homilies. But occurring where they did in Hasidism and placed as they are in Buber's restoration of the essential Hasidic development, they make the point that neither the meaning nor the temptations of the 'go it alone' aspect of Abraham's calling were lost on the true zaddiks.

* * *

We had occasion to resort, in the last chapter, to H. G. Wells' outline for a modern Noachic view of history. It is therefore interesting to find him quoted in a discussion of separatism in a book on *Judaism as Creed and Life*.[20] 'The Jew', Wells wrote, 'will probably lose much of his particularism, intermarry with Gentiles, and cease to be a physically distinct element in human affairs. But much of his moral tradition will, I hope, never die.' A rather more universal fate, on the same lines, has been forecast for the Jews by the historian Arnold Toynbee, who would have the Jews as such assimilate and their 'ethical monotheism' conquer the world. If it is to do so, one understands, the Jews had better vanish quickly from the scene. On this sort of evaporation of dedicated living religion into liberal idealism with just a dash of metaphysics, no comment is required in a book on Martin Buber.

Others have suspected that Jewish separatism has survived only because the Jews in Europe could hardly have existed without it. Hostility, persecution and extinction were lavished upon them from all sides. But, as a Jewish historian[21] has pointed out: 'Long before residence within a restricted quarter or ghetto was compulsory, the Jews almost everywhere had concentrated in separate parts of the towns in which they lived.' When it was no longer also socially necessary to do so, the inner power of Jewish religious life waned and the brilliant attractions of the Enlightenment beckoned, increasing numbers of Jews turned to the path that led to assimilation. The German experience of what it might mean to be a Jew in a society which recognized (quite correctly, in a way not clear to Adolf Hitler) the Jew as committed to 'universal conspiracy' has prompted others to seek assimilation, or at any rate protective colouration, as some sort of insurance for survival.

Very little was known of the allurements and perils of the Enlightenment in the poverty-stricken Eastern Europe in which Hasidism arose, but its essential appeal to Jewish spiritual experience as well as, and not instead of, traditional Jewish procedures, was nevertheless the real Jewish answer to the way the Western world was going. And whereas nature came to mean less and less to urban Noachic man, the land, any land—since it too was part of the creation—was a joy to the father of Hasidism, the Baal Shem Tov. Schecter[22] points the contrast between the two elements in Judaism at the time in a few words in which it is significant that we get an almost paradisal glimpse of the land, the Polish land stained dark with Jewish blood:

> The hero of the Polish Rabbinic biography at five years of age can recite by heart the most difficult tractates of the Talmud; at eight he is the disciple of the most celebrated teacher of the time, and perplexes him by the penetrative subtlety of his questions; while at thirteen he appears before the world as a full-fledged Doctor of the Law.
>
> The hero of Hasidism has a totally different education, and his distinctive glory is of another kind. The legendary stories

about Baalshem's youth tell us little of his proficiency in Talmudic studies; instead of sitting in the Beth Hamidrash with the folios of some casuistic treatise spread out before him, Baalshem passes his time singing hymns out of doors, or under the green trees of the forest with the children. Satan, however, says the Hasid, is more afraid of these innocent exercises than all the controversies in the Maharam Shiff.

It is difficult not to agree with Satan.

* * *

However, the reader who relishes Schecter's sketch of the Baal Shem as a youth enjoying the countryside and would settle for that with, perhaps, just a dash of Wordsworthian nature mysticism for religious respectability, will find the depths opening up under his feet if he turns to Hasidic legends about the Abrahamic seed in the Jewish soul which yearns for the Land itself. The wholeness and righteousness of the zaddik, for whom the journey to Jerusalem is neither a trip nor a removal to simply congenial surroundings, or yet a utopian political experiment, but the outward gesture of a spiritual pilgrimage of the most exacting kind, will not here be separately discussed. But their presence is what makes the difference between a biographical episode and a Hasidic 'legend' in the exemplary case of the great-grandson of the Baal Shem Tov.

In introducing his first treatment of *The Legend of the Baal Shem*, Buber makes an important distinction between classical myth and legend, as he employs that term in his early work:

> In pure myth there is no division of essential being. It knows multiplicity but not duality. Even the hero stands on another rung than that of the god, not over against him: they are not the I and the Thou. The hero has a mission but not a call. He ascends but he does not become transformed. The god of pure myth does not call, he begets; he sends forth the one whom he begets, the hero. The god of the legend calls forth the son of man—the prophet, the holy man.[23]

Later, of course, Buber redeems 'myth' from such pagan connotation and uses it of the Biblical treatment of the archetypal and patriarchal figures. The distinction remains useful, and we

now use 'legend' for tales of exceptional men in their encounters
with divine reality, men beneath the level of the great Biblical
figures but still far above the average of Jewish mankind. It may
be noted that Buber modestly indicates the two elements in his
own Hasidic work by describing *For the Sake of Heaven* as 'in the
the form of a novel, or more correctly, a chronicle'.[24] That is, it
too combines the mystery of the organic memory with the
verifiable historic event. *For the Sake of Heaven*, if it is a novel,
raises that art from from the novel to the genuinely new.

* * *

The Jew of the Diaspora was not only separated from the nations,
he was also expelled from his own holy land. He was apart from
everything but God and his fellow Jews and the 'unredeemed'
nature around him. But for the Hasid, and still more for the
zaddik, what this hostile or at least alien environment spoke to
him was an incessant reminder of the inner journey of which the
outer one, with all its challenges and perils, of a return to Zion
was the expression and completion.

So much is given and implied by Martin Buber in the section
of *Israel and Palestine* that gives the legend of Rabbi Nachman's
actual journey to the Holy Land and return to Poland, that it is
necessary to emphasize here that only enough of it will be discussed to sustain the thesis of this book—which is that Martin
Buber's interpretation of the Bible is reflected in his understanding of Hasidism and also in his formulation in the modern terms
of the I–Thou 'philosophy'—enough, it is hoped, to tempt the
reader to turn to the source itself. He should turn also to Buber's
beautiful restoration of *The Tales of Rabbi Nachman*.

> In Rabbi Nachman of Brazlaw, the great-grandson of the
> Baal Shem Tov, the founder of Hasidism, everything was
> gathered together and concentrated, with and also without
> his knowledge, that the generations of the Diaspora had
> felt, dreamt and thought about the land of Israel. He must
> be seen as the great heir, who uses his inheritance mag-
> nanimously. It is characteristic of his nature and his mission
> that he became, without any literary ambitions of any kind,
> simply through oral intercourse with his disciples, the
> creator of a literary genre, the symbolical fairy-tale, but that

in this new form age-old treasures of mystic tradition were assimilated and endowed with a supreme splendour. He is the best example possible of the relationship of the Hasidic movement to Palestine: everything flows together in him and everything finds exemplary expression in his life and words.[25]

But before the story can be told Buber has to take into account the spiritual dangers of Messianism with which 'the journey to Jerusalem' in its outward, as well as—of course—in its inward sense was then threatened. To this explosive but unavoidable theme we shall turn in the final chapter, where we shall consider Buber's appreciation of Jesus. We cannot here consider Buber's treatments of what prevented the Baal Shem Tov himself from travelling to the Holy Land as he purposed, though without them the significance of certain incidents in the legend of Rabbi Nachman's journey are almost indecipherable. The impressive thing is that such intimate and unspeakable events of spiritual striving can be evoked at all. But this is unquestionably achieved in Martin Buber's handling of Hasidic legendary material, and is perhaps the most impressive vindication we have of what this form, as distinct from the work of analytical intelligence, can communicate to the responsive and attentive reader.

The great resources of the soul in peril on this journey are prayer and sacrifice. Here again we shall need to turn to what is indicated in Buber's narration of Rabbi Nachman's journey, to throw some light on the place of prayer in the life of the Hasidim, in the chapter which will consider his treatment of the Psalmist.

The Rabbi learns in the night from the spirit of his great-grandfather that, in preparation for his journey, he is to travel to the city of Kamieniec:

> Of his sojourn in Kamieniec it is reported that he spent the night alone in the city where Jews were forbidden to live and that thereafter the ban was lifted. He himself said later, whoever knows why the land of Israel was first in the hands of the Canaanites and did not come into Israel's hands until afterwards ('the skin had to precede the fruit,' as he says in one of his didactic speeches) also knows why he was in Kamieniec before he travelled into the land of Israel. It was therefore a symbolical action that he stayed the night in the

Jewless city, before he set out for the land promised to Israel, and it was precisely this action that he understood the Baal-Shem to have commanded him to perform. Before he set out for Miedzyborz, he had stated that he himself did not know whither he was travelling. By sending him to Kamieniec, his great-grandfather shows him the way he was to go.[26]

To offer to 'interpret' this would be insensitive and impertinent. But it is fairly evident that the discovery of his own essential Jewishness in the darkened city where no other Jew was suffered to remain is related to the archetype of Abraham's experience in Ur. Buber's interpolated citation of the fruit that grows unseen of any living eye *within* the skin that differs from it, suggesting the splitting of the skin at natural ripeness, intimates with his typical reticent tenderness the character of the inner experience which make possible the first step on the long and perilous way.

*   *   *

In a certain sense it may perhaps be said that the Noachic man expires when the Abrahamic man is born in a person. Passing over the whole legend of the journey, the eventful sojourn and the return—Rabbi Nachman finally avoided Jerusalem—it concerns us here to notice how only after all this and nearing the end of the relation, the name we are waiting for appears quietly on the page for the first and only time:

> We have heard that the resurrection of the dead will have its centre in the land of Israel. That is why the tomb achieves its perfect form here; here alone is the place of perfect burial. For the reason why death has been imposed on man is known to tradition: it is because in the sin of the first man a defilement by the serpent invaded our imagination from which we can be perfectly cleansed in no other way than by the death of the body. In a proper death and a proper burial the impurity is dissolved and a new body will arise in a renewed world. All this, however, is perfectly achieved only in the land of Israel. For the overcoming of the defiled imagination occurs through faith, but the power of faith has implanted itself in this land and lives and works therein.

Abraham, the father of faith, was the first to reveal this holy power when he acquired the burial-place of the cave of Makhpela.[27]

This kind of language is not, perhaps, to everybody's taste. Some may consider it 'legend' in a derogatory sense. To speak for once in the first person, let me say, I, a Gentile to whom the language is unknown, take it for good Hebrew.

* * *

The temptation to lapse, and for the purpose of this book it would indeed be a fatal lapse, from the attempt to find concepts that build the indispensable bridge to myth, as Buber understands myth, into the relative security of an intellectual system that could aspire to dominate and order 'the facts' assails us here in full strength. We can accept, perhaps, the far away and long ago fable of the 'straying Aramean' (as Buber translates the 'wandering Aramean' of the Masoretic rendering of Deuteronomy 26:5) who mysteriously became a wayfaring Hebrew, no longer Abram but Abraham, and imagine the scenery of the land to which he is directed and which he claims for God. We can be at least intrigued by the mysteries of Rabbi Nachman's journey to the land, as some sort of post-Kabbalistic Jewish thriller. But now that we come to our own time and the men who returned to the land, surely we must have done with myth? Or at the very least, if we are to romance a little about a recent hero, the natural background with its rich historical associations can be no more than that?

The temptation, then, is to argue, or rather lay down basic theological propositions. There is God. There is man, or rather men. There is the world. God created the men and the world. There is something, call it divine purpose in history, to be worked out not merely between the first two, but between all three of these components. The bringing of them all into harmony is called true dialogue. *Therefore*, there must be dialogue between God and man? Granted. And between man and man? Granted. And between man and 'nature'? Consternation. Words fail us here, we say, as *words* are irrelevant to our relation with our natural environment.

When Martin Buber added a postscipt to the second edition of *I and Thou*,[28] the first thing he had to deal with was: what could he possibly mean by saying that man can have relationship not only with 'spiritual beings' (whatever that might mean it was still religiously respectable) with his fellow man (relatively plain sailing this, it was supposed) but with—as he had said in the book, *a tree*![29] This encounter with a tree is not a random example. It is autobiographical, and forms the opening of the Author's Preface to his early work *Daniel*.[30] 'At that time dialogue appeared to me.' It does not easily appear to the general reader.

The reason is, perhaps, threefold. The modern city-dweller is very much the town mouse and not the country mouse. He has largely lost his sense of the rhythm of the seasons, seed-time and harvest, of the *adamah* (earth) as the very stuff from which the *adam* (man) was formed and on whose fruitfulness under the sun and rain of the blue and white sky depends the physical possibility of his being able to be fruitful and multiply. Then—and if Buber can be said to be fierce about anything he is fierce against this—we have split off 'religion' into a separate compartment, into which nature is admitted once a year at some kind of harvest festival. Worst of all, religion itself has become loftily 'otherworldly'. Redemption is strictly for human beings, usually selected ones at that, and nature is quite out of it. No wonder Martin Buber communing with a tree could raise a highly civilized smile on many faces. World food production is, of course, a problem; raw materials must be wrested from the earth to feed the industrial machine, at least until we can replace them all with new synthetics. But let us get this straight. The world is a thing, there for our use, and (except for that charming traditional harvest festival once a year, when it decorates the church so nicely) it has no part in redemption.

*   *   *

The story of Abraham, which connects the gift of Canaan with the command to be a blessing, is a most concise resumé of the fact that the association of this people with this land signifies a mission. The people came to the land to fulfil the mission, even by each new revolt against it they recognized its continuing validity; the prophets were appointed to interpret the past and future destiny of the people on the basis of its failure as yet to establish the righteous city of God for the establishment of which it had been led into the land. This land was at no time in the history of Israel simply the property of the people; it was always at the same time a challenge to make of it what God intended to have made of it.

Thus from the very beginning the unique association between this people and this land was characterized by what was to be, by the intention that was to be realized. It was a consummation that could not be achieved by the people or the land on its own but only by the faithful co-operation of the two together and it was an association in which the land appeared not as a dead, passive object but as a living and active partner. Just as, to achieve fullness of life, the people needed the land, so the land needed the people, and the end which both were called upon to realize could only be reached by a living partnership. Since the living land shared the great work with the living people it was to be both the work of history and the work of nature. Just as nature and history were united in the creation of man, so these two spheres which have become separated in the human mind were to unite in the task in which the chosen land and the chosen people were called upon to co-operate. The holy matrimony of land and people was intended to bring about the matrimony of the two separated spheres of Being.[31]

That is from the Introduction to *Israel and Palestine*, written there in 1944. The book concludes with the modern 'myth' of 'A Man Who Realizes the Idea of Zion'.[32] The man was Ahron David Gordon and he came from what may be called the Hasidic heartland, a Podolian village:

a man like Gordon is exceptional in that he seems to associate directly with the powers of Nature and not merely indirectly by way of social forms. This is an occurrence of extraordinary rarity in the Jewish people.[33]

The real wound in Gordon's heart is caused by the Jews having fallen not from political self-determination but from the Cosmos. No merely receptive behaviour will enable them to find their place in it again. Man can participate in the Cosmos only when he *does* something in the cosmic context that is his particular sphere, just as the stars revolve

in their courses and the trees grow towards the sun. To work
on the land entrusted to his care is what befits man. The
men sent by a newly arising Israel to work on the soil of its
land represent its reunion, not merely with the earth but
with the Cosmos.[34]

Even Tolstoy, Buber feels, did not see in the relationship
between man and earth the problem of man's gaining his place
in the Cosmos. Whitman and Thoreau are wandering gloriously
with nature and if Thoreau takes a hand on the farm he does not
know *what* he is doing. Wordsworthian contemplation does not
come in for mention here at all.

Buber brings out the stages of Gordon's relationship to the
holy land in three phases each separated by five years. After the
first five years

'The land of my fathers is far and strange to me and I am
far and strange to it.'

But he also sees that

'The devastation . . . *is* the devastation of your soul and
the corrupter is the corrupter who has ruled in your life . . .
you stand before your own fate.'[35]

Five years later, at the beginning of World War I:

'The mother Erets Israel . . . claims your body and life or
she claims nothing. It is not my purpose to direct your
attention to what you should and could do for Palestine,
but to what Palestine can do for you . . . Only when you
begin to look for something that no Jew can find anywhere
else . . . only then will you be competent to do something,
something of vital importance for Palestine.[36]

Five more years go by, and Buber sees Gordon for the first and
last time, in Prague:

'It is not we,' he says, 'it is our land, that speaks to the
people. We have merely to express and intimate the words
spoken by the land, and we say to you, to the whole people:
the land is waiting for you.'[37]

Not only the exile but the land too had decayed with the

long separation. The struggle was hard. Gordon wrote in a letter
that:

> 'We have only *one* comfort ... that we feel our pains
> thoroughly. We are like a woman, who for a long time had
> no children, however much she besought God—and who
> suddenly notices that she is pregnant. She rejoices over every
> pain and only fears that the pain may be too light, since
> perhaps it is not the real pain. In the Diaspora we did not
> feel *these* pains.'[38]

And Buber adds:

> With this very metaphor, a Hasidic leader, Rabbi Israel of
> Rizin had once spoken of the redemption.

*　　*　　*

We began this chapter by quoting Martin Buber's vindication
of the true marriage of the historical and the mythic which
constitutes the Biblical. We noted that the Hasidic marriage of
the marvellous and the actual was of the same lineage. We
suggested that Buber's novel-cum-chronicle was, too. The 'facts'
without the real experience of them are I–It. The true intercourse
between event and man is I–Thou. This is not a literary tradition
or a school of thought. In the Bible, reality is presented to us as
'a doctrine which is nothing but history, and as a history which is
nothing but doctrine'.[39]

The real heresy is to suppose that this is not still true of reality
today and every day, here and now, as well as far away and long
ago. Miracle is simply a true way of seeing what happens. It is
time that we visited this declaration of faith on Buber himself.
We know by now how deeply he took the call for 'wholeness' as
the correspondence of the inner and the outer. We cannot believe
that he could write of the Baal Shem's Messianic temptation, of
his frustrated longing to go to the Holy Land, of his great-
grandson's journey marked with spiritual perils and adventures
—and then pack his bags early in 1938 merely to depart for the
Hebrew University in Jerusalem to pursue an academic career
undisturbed by events in Europe.

We are not told directly anything of his inner life at that
crucial time. I say directly because whoever reads what he wrote

of the Baal Shem and Rabbi Nachman and takes it for something like 'brilliant imaginative reconstruction' is unfit to read such books. The other thing we can do is to see this homing flight against the whole catastrophic panorama of the history of our time. In the year after Buber left Europe, the Continent plunged into total War and little Poland, in particular, was rent asunder once more. Something like one-third of the Jews of the world, many of whom had gone to a greater or less extent the way of the world, were destroyed far from any field of battle. At that time the future of Palestine was unknown. Within a decade of Buber's arrival, the State of Israel reappeared on the map of the world for the first time in nearly two thousand years. Can anyone look steadily at this true picture and not feel, against all non-Biblical explanations of the movements of history and the life of man, a beyond-reason stirring of the myth in the event?

Let the unprejudiced reader, who does not mistake Martin Buber's writing for 'literature' in the limited sense of that word, consider what is expressed in the apparently bibliographical paragraph that concludes the Preface to *Tales of the Hasidim: The Early Masters*, dated *Jerusalem*, Summer 1946:

> My work of re-telling hasidic legends began more than forty years ago. Its first fruits were the books entitled 'Tales of Rabbi Nachman' (1906), and 'The Legend of the Baal Shem' (1907). Subsequently, however, I rejected my method of dealing with the transmitted material, on the grounds that it was too free. I applied my new concept of the task and the means to accomplish it, in the books 'The Great Maggid and His Succession' (1921) and 'The Hidden Light' (1924). The content of these two books has been reproduced almost entirely in this book, but by far the greater part of it was written since my arrival in Palestine in 1938. Along with much else, I owe the urge to this new and more comprehensive composition to the air of this land. Our sages say that it makes one wise; to me it has granted a different gift: the strength to make a new beginning. I had regarded my work on the hasidic legends as completed. This book is the outcome of a beginning.[40]

And the Introduction begins with the short sentence:

The purpose of this book is to introduce the reader to a world of legendary reality.[41]

To avoid misunderstanding, the present writer must add that no more but no less is here claimed for Martin Buber than that he is entitled to be recognized as a true representative in our time of Abrahamic man.

THE WAYFARING PEOPLE: MOSES

BEFORE man and earth can come together in a way that gives man a legitimate standing over against the Cosmos, which he no longer seeks merely to enslave, erode and exploit but wishes to nurture—as Nature's Abrahamic cell, so to say—from wilderness to paradise, he must encounter the Creator through his creation. Let us be plain about this too. If prophecy—in the fullest sense of the term—has ceased since four centuries before the beginning of the Common Era, we must take it less that God no longer addresses individual men than that men no longer go out to the supreme encounter. Potentially, the encounter might occur to any Abrahamic man at any time, in any place; indeed, in some degree it does so. But though the 'talk' of Nature is of nothing else, it is mostly talk—Nature's behaviour leaves as much to be desired as man's, as one may see from any cat among the pigeons. It is seldom that a man can apprehend it and rare indeed that he feels the actual encounter to the full limit of his own united being. Martin Buber is not deluded when he feels some mutuality between himself and the tree. Moses, who like Abel has become a keeper of sheep, hears a 'voice' from a thorn bush whose mysteriously enhanced reality in its relation with him can be expressed only by saying that it burned and was not consumed.

The conclusion, which the most ardent intellectualist will hardly suppose that Moses rightly reasoned out but by which he was overwhelmed, is that God—we mean what has become a flippancy to signify the mythic but otherwise quite sober truth—can show up anywhere at any time; for instance, here and now. So that His true Name can only be, as Moses—to whom it is first disclosed—apprehends the communication, and as Martin Buber translates: I WILL BE PRESENT AS EVER I WILL BE PRESENT.[1]

As reply to his question about the name Moses is told: *Ehyeh asher ehyeh*. This is usually understood to mean 'I am that I am' in the sense that YHVH describes himself as the

Being One or even the Everlasting One, the one un-
alterably persisting in his being. But that would be abstraction of a kind which does not usually come about in periods
of increasing religious vitality; while in addition the verb in
the Biblical language does not carry this particular shade of
meaning of pure existence. It means: happening, coming
into being, being there, being present, being thus and thus;
but not being in an abstract sense. 'I am that I am' could
only be understood as an avoiding of the question, as a
'statement which withholds information'. Should we, however, really assume that in the view of the narrator the God
who came to inform His people of their liberation wishes, at
that hour of all hours, merely to secure His distance, and not
to grant and warrant proximity as well?[2]

In this great work on *Moses*, Buber also adverts to the first
prophet's apprehension of the One God who is as yet nameless:

The God by whom Abraham, after 'straying away' from
Haran, is led in his wanderings, differs from all solar, lunar
and stellar divinities, apart from the fact that He guides only
Abraham and His own group, by the further fact that He is
not regularly visible in the heavens, but only occasionally
permits Himself to be seen by His chosen; whenever and
wherever it is His will to do so. This necessarily implies that
various natural things and processes are on occasion
regarded as manifestations of the God, and that it is impossible to know for certain where or wherein He will next
appear.[3]

There is no contrast between Abraham's experience of God,
which is pre-nomian, before the giving of the Law, and Moses'
experience of God, before he becomes the great promulgator of
the Law.

Moses' revelation at the burning bush precedes, of course, the
exodus and the giving of the Law. It will be clear that, in giving
us his renovated understanding of the Name itself Buber is taking
his supreme stand. Everything else he says will be in relation to
this acceptance of the Name. So that nothing can, for him, limit
this revelation of God's ubiquity and of the unpredictability of
His manifestations. Not even, as we shall see, in the extreme case

of killing. This is what the world calls antinomianism, if it does
not call it anarchy. It is encouraging to those who, holding that
the Law passed away with the advent of Jesus, consider Buber,
whose love for Jesus is certainly not hidden, as a kind of Christian
unawares. We had better anticipate the final chapter for a
moment, by seeing how Buber clears up that point in an address
to four German missions to the Jews:

> You have asked me to speak to you about the soul of Judaism.
> I have complied with this request, although I am against the
> cause for which you hold your conference, and I am against
> it not 'just as a Jew', but also truly as a Jew, that is, as one
> who waits for the Kingdom of God, the Kingdom of
> Unification, and who regards all such 'missions' as yours as
> springing from a misunderstanding of that kingdom, and as
> a hindrance to its coming.[4]

And then, directly:

> I do not feel myself called upon to speak before you (about)
> 'the Law'. My point of view with regard to this subject
> diverges from the traditional one: it is not a-nomistic, but
> neither is it entirely nomistic.[5]

We must here listen with the utmost care. To the possible
reproach, to which he does not refer, that he is actually opposed
to the Law, he returns no answer, as such a man may do when
most deeply, however unintentionally, insulted. To the possible
misunderstanding that he is indifferent or somehow 'neutral' to
the Law he answers categorically: no. But to the demand that he
should be 'entirely' nomistic—that he should accept the Law,
the whole Law and nothing but the Law—he demurs. And why?
Nahum Glatzer[6] found the right abstract word for Buber's profoundly religious position: metanomianism, the law of the spirit
of God. It is, of course, a supremely dangerous way. But no one
ventures to impugn courage.

The primary encounters with God by Abraham and Moses
also precede the making of the Ark of the Covenant, which stands
around and above the tablets of the Law. If the God who might
manifest anywhere, the God who 'went before' the Israelites in
the wilderness, the God who 'spoke' from Sinai, seems finally to

have come to rest in one terrestial place, first in the middle of the camp and then eventually in the Temple at Jerusalem, that is rather for Buber the supreme limit of intimation to limited men—and all are limited to a greater or less extent—of how *to the Abrahamic awareness* the veritable Presence is to be ceaselessly sought in every here and now, and the search need never be in vain, if God so wills. The Ark is the tangible fountain-head of myth, of Biblical awareness of reality. That is its essential difference from the 'Golden Calf'—which guarantees a specific localization and no other.

> We have no reliable reports as to the original appearance of the Ark. If, as it seems to me may be assumed, the cherubim were already part of it, then we have to distinguish between them as the actual seat of the throne and the shrine as the foot-stool of the throne; as was expressly done later for the Ark introduced into the temple of Solomon. The heavenly beings have flown down, so to say, in order to prepare for YHVH the seat of the throne on which He descends when He desires; for this, the fact that He sometimes descends thereon, is what is meant by the descriptive term 'Who is seated upon the cherubim' . . .[7]

Here we must directly quote Scripture:[8]

> And the LORD spoke unto Moses . . . 'And thou shalt make two cherubim of gold; of beaten work shalt thou make them, at the two ends of the ark-cover. And make one cherub at the one end, and one cherub at the other end; of one piece with the ark-cover shall ye make the cherubim of the two ends thereof. And the cherubim shall spread out their wings on high, screening the ark-cover with their wings, with their faces one to another; toward the ark-cover shall the faces of the cherubim be. And thou shalt put the ark-cover above upon the ark; and in the ark thou shalt put the testimony that I shall give thee. And there I will meet with thee, and I will speak with thee from above the ark-cover, from between the two cherubim which are upon the ark of the testimony, of all things which I will give thee in commandment unto the children of Israel.'

The voice from 'between' the cherubim is above the Law.

Now—we may remark—we can begin to appreciate why Jonathan says to David,[9] whom he loved 'as he loved his own soul'[10]—to David who was to dance in the street as he brought the Ark into Jerusalem[11]—'And as touching the matter which I and thou have spoken of, behold the LORD is between me and thee for ever.' We may also have found the Biblical root of Martin Buber's essential vocabulary: *I and Thou*; *Between Man and Man*. We may think, too, of the work of the Bible that was between Martin Buber and Franz Rosenzweig.

*   *   *

It must be repeated. This book is dedicated to the purpose of tracing 'The Hebrew Tradition in the Writings of Martin Buber'. It is not intended as polemic. In particular, it is not written to join issue with any part of the Jewish—or for that matter the Christian—community. Least of all is it intended to be anti-rabbinic. The writer might indeed improve a little on the familiar cliché and protest that some of his best friends are rabbis, and not of the far Left either. So it is only right to mention that 'It would be unfair to characterize the lifework of the Talmudic Rabbins as that of "binding" only . . . they roundly declared in general terms that there were circumstances in which to suspend the laws of the Torah was to fulfil it.'[12] (Menachoth, 99b). Indeed, not merely to suspend but to annul. The popular antithesis of Law and Spirit, in which, of course, all right-minded men of goodwill are loudly on the side of the spirit, will not here be used as a stick to beat the rabbinate. Nor does Buber anywhere so use it.

At the same time, we cannot fairly turn to the Hasidic phase of our Mosaic theme without remarking that the form, and often the extreme and disorderly form, taken by Hasidism in the eighteenth century, which evoked a very sharp reaction from the Law-upholding orthodox rabbis, can be fairly judged only by recording the view of most Jewish authorities that excessive legalism was rampant at the time. The Hasidim did not rebel against the Law but they accused their opponents of enforcing its minutiae without the proper sptrilual inwardness; and they tended to regulate their own pious observance by an unpredictable spirituality rather than *vice versa*. There were, in short, faults on both sides. The essay by Solomon Schecter, from which we have already quoted, may be acceptable to most readers as tolerably near the middle of the road:

> By the service of God was generally understood a life which fulfilled the precepts of the written and oral law. Baal-Shem understood by it a certain attitude towards life as a whole. For, as God is realized in life, each activity of life when rightly conceived and executed is at once a manifestation and a service of the Divine . . . For when the Torah had once been given by God the whole world became instinct with its grace. He who speaks of worldly matters and religious matters as if they were separate and distinct, is a heretic.
>
> Upon the continual and uninterrupted study of the Law, Baal-Shem lays but little stress. He accepted the ordinary belief that the Law . . . was a revelation of God. But, as the world itself is equally a divine revelation, the Torah becomes little more than a part of a larger whole. To understand it aright one needs to penetrate to the inward reality—to the infinite light which is revealed in it . . . Thus the study of the law is no end in itself . . .
>
> The object of the whole Torah is that man should become a Torah himself. Every man being a Torah in himself, said a disciple of Baal-Shem, has got not only his Abraham and Moses, but also his Balaam and Haman; he should try to expel the Balaam and develop the Abraham within him. Every action of man should be a pure manifestation of God.[13]

Thus generally characterized, it is easy for anyone of even moderate experience to see the attractions and the perils. Just as the stricter dogmatics and disciplines of the Catholic Church led to the Protestant revolt, that in turn to the relatively latitudinarian Free Churches—all in the name of the spirit against the letter—so the further step that has now been taken by a large proportion of the Western people is into a frankly a-religious paganism of 'it doesn't matter what you do, so long as you don't harm anyone else'. Why it has somehow come about that this seems to be a matter of jiving—there is nothing intrinsically wrong with jiving any more than there was in Adam eating a fruit he fancied—while the world burns, the new paganism does not altogether comprehend. But as the H-bomb is distributed among the rival nations and the possibility of universal annihilation grows, it is at least possible to wonder if Martin Buber's teaching, that the alternative to *the* way is a wandering that leads literally into nothingness, is not worth considering. It is therefore important to enquire: does he really open the gates of true Judaism to a go-as-you-please attitude, only the more intolerable because it may be presented in highly plausible spiritual poses?

Buber has been in trouble with learned critics for being selective in his presentation of Hasidism. He is concerned with its pure essence, and the joyous community life that sprang from it. The difference between antinomianism and metanomianism comes out quite distinctively in a single example from *Tales of the Hasidim: The Later Masters:*[14]

> A disciple asked Rabbi Mendel of Rymanov: 'The Talmud says that Abraham fulfilled all the commandments. How is that possible, since they had not yet been given?' 'You know,' said the rabbi, 'that the commandments of the Torah correspond to the bones, and the prohibitions to the sinews of man. Thus the entire Law includes the entire body of man. But Abraham made every part of his body so pure and holy that each of itself fulfilled the command intended for it.'

True Hasidism, it is clear, was not a teaching of just being jolly, sociable and helpful and not bothering too much about the rules and regulations. It was certainly no less strenuous than the form of observance which, outwardly, might be contrasted with it. And in fact Hasidism was, with some irregularities, fairly observant, and was finally reconciled with orthodox practice on that score.

We need add only one more note to this brief glance at Buber's treatment of the metanomian attitude in essential Hasidism, in which, as the disciple of the Baal-Shem was quoted as saying, he has his Abraham and his Moses, and is not unaware of the presence of less desirable Biblical characters in himself besides. Martin Buber's collected *Werke* have lately appeared in three volumes:

> Erster Band: Schriften zur Philosophie
> Zweiter Band: Schriften zur Bibel
> Dritter Band, Schriften zum Chassidismus

Even one who has no German can read this. Between Martin Buber's own teaching and that of the Baal Shem Tov is his interpretation of the Hebrew Bible. One thinks again of Rosenzweig and Buber, of Jonathan and David, and of the golden cherubim; and of what was between them.

* * *

As Rosenzweig saw it, the situation of the Jew in relation to the Law in his own time was calamitous. We cannot do better than quote Nahum Glatzer's appraisal of the situation:

> The treatise *The Builders* (*Die Bauleute*) written in the summer of 1923 and addressed to Martin Buber, takes the fateful step from Jewish knowledge to Halakhah, the commandments and their observance. Western Judaism after the Emancipation (outside of authoritarian, fundamentalists, Orthodoxy) reduced the wide scope of the Law to 'rituals and customs', sancta of the Jewish people, or just folkways. It ceased to be a problem of Jewish religion. 'Revelation' could take on no new theological or philosophical meaning; the 'Law' was no longer understood as the expressed will of God and was—theoretically at least—considered obsolete. A law-free, antinomian attitude, which earlier periods in Judaism arrived at after mighty convulsions in the soul of the people, was uncritically accepted as a natural development in modern times.[15]

The Builders led to the renewal in 1924 of a correspondence between Buber and Rosenzweig begun in 1922. We must resist the temptation to follow it closely. It is important here for one reason. Martin Buber has not cared to discuss his personal religious life in public, but he would not limit this private exchange with Rosenzweig to assertion and interpretation. He had to make his friend understand his position from his own life. That Buber permitted the publication of these letters thirty years later is but one more expression of his regard for his dead friend, whose own correspondence would not have been fully understood without them.

Already in 1922 he related how his father took him to

> the Temple (sic!) in Lemberg, where I went only when my father wished to lure me away from my grandfather who

liked to take me to a small hasidic *Klaus*. He, an 'enlightened' Jew, a Maskil, liked to pray among the Hasidim and
used a prayer book full of mystical directions . . .[16]

In this liberal synagogue at Lemberg—

> . . . on a Day of Atonement I caused annoyance . . . by
> following the tradition of bending my knee and prostrating
> myself while reciting the words, 'We bend our knee and
> prostrate ourselves . . .'[17]

This wholly characteristic suiting of the action to the word,
the completion of a genuine 'inner' with the corresponding
'outer' action was not welcome. But if Buber's way of observance
can no longer be mistaken for 'exhibitionism' it is hardly to be
supposed that its inwardness is less deep than in his youth or that
it finds no outward correlative. It is some time, perhaps, before
the general reader begins to appreciate the wholeness and
intensity with which Buber stands behind every word he speaks
and writes. Beneath its sobriety is an intensity that makes it one
of the noblest 'styles' of our time.

Again, writing to Rosenzweig late in 1922, he says:

> But I must still tell you something serious: that in spite of
> everything, I feel in my innermost heart that today is the
> Eve of Yom Kippur. This may be so because (if I may add
> an autobiographical note) between my thirteenth and
> fourteenth year (when I was fourteen I stopped putting on
> my Tefillin) I experienced this day with a force unequalled
> by any other experience since. And do you think that I was
> a 'child' at that time? Maybe less so than now, and this in a
> poignant sense; at that time I took Space and Time
> seriously; I did not hold back as I do now. And then, when
> the sleepless night was heavy upon me and very real, my
> body, already reacting to the fast, became as important to
> me as an animal marked for sacrifice. This is what formed
> me: the night and the following morning, and the Day
> itself, with all its hours, not omitting a single moment.[18]

And in 1924, of the first of the observances, the Sabbath:

> I told you that for me, though man is a law-receiver, God
> is not a law-giver, and therefore the Law has no universal
> validity for me, but only a personal one. I accept, therefore,

only what I think is being spoken to me (e.g., the older I become, and the more I realize the restlessness of my soul, the more I accept for myself the Day of Rest).[19]

*　　*　　*

It was several years later that someone sent Martin Buber a circular containing the question, 'What Are We To Do About the Ten Commandments?'

You want to know what I think should be done about the Ten Commandments in order to give them a sanction and validity they no longer possess.

In my opinion the historical and present status of the Decalogue derives from a twofold fact.

(1) The Ten Commandments are not part of an impersonal codex governing an association of men. They were uttered by an *I* and addressed to a *Thou*. They begin with the *I* and every one of them addresses the *Thou* in person. An *I* 'commands' and a *Thou*—every *Thou* who hears this *Thou* 'is commanded'.

(2) In the Decalogue, the word of Him who issues commands is equipped with no executive power effective on the plane of predictable causality. The word does not enforce its own hearing. Whoever does not wish to respond to the Thou addressed to him can apparently go about his business unimpeded. Though He who speaks the word has power (and the Decalogue presupposes that He had sufficient power to create the heavens and the earth) He has renounced this power of his sufficiently to let every individual actually decide for himself whether he wants to choose or reject that I of 'I am'. He who rejects Him is not struck down by lightning; he who elects Him does not find hidden treasures. Everything seems to remain just as it was. Obviously God does not wish to dispense either medals or prison sentences.[20]

He then points out that 'Faith is not a mere business enterprise which involves risk balanced by the possibility of incalculable gain'—whether before death or after—'it is the venture pure and simple, a venture which transcends the law of probability'. But society has its own idea about command and law:

Now human society, and by that I mean the living community at any definite period, as far as we can recognize the existence of a common will in its institutions, has at all times had an interest in fostering and keeping the Ten Commandments. It was, to be sure, less interested in those commandments which refer to the relationship to God, but it certainly wants the rest to be kept, because it would not be conducive to the welfare of society if murder, for example, ceased to be a crime and became a vice. To a certain extent this holds even for the prohibition against adultery, at least as long as society believes that it cannot get along without marriage, and indeed it never has gotten along without it, not even in its 'primitive' stages of polyandry and polygamy. And as long as society cares about maintaining the connection between generations and transmitting forms and contents in a well-regulated manner, it must respect the command to honour one's parents. The Soviet Union has proven that even a society built up to achieve communistic goals must care about honouring that commandment.

The searching irony now turns to direct challenge:

It is understandable that society does not want to base so vital a matter on so insecure a foundation as faith—on wanting or not wanting to hear. So, society has always endeavoured to transfer those commands and prohibitions it considered important from the sphere of '*religion*' to that of '*morals*', to translate them from the language which uses the personal imperative to the impersonal formulation of 'musts'. Society wishes these commandments to be upheld by public opinion, which can to a certain extent be controlled, rather than by the will of God whose effectiveness cannot be predicted or counted on. But since even the security of opinion is not entirely dependable, the commands and prohibitions are once more transferred, this time to the sphere of 'law', i.e., they are translated into the language of if-formulations: 'If someone should do this or that, then such and such a thing shall be done to him.' And the purpose of the threat of 'such and such a thing' is not to limit the freedom of action of the law-breaker, but to punish him.

God scorned to regulate the relation between what a man does and what, as a result of his doing, is done to him, by exact mathematical rules, but that is exactly what society attempts. To be sure, society certainly *has* the personnel to carry out its rulings, a personnel which, at least in principle, has well-defined work to perform: the courts, the police, jailers and hangmen. Oddly enough, however, the result is still far from satisfactory. Statistics, for example do not show that the death penalty has had the effect of diminishing the number of murders.[21]

He had, he confessed, oversimplified for the sake of clarity. But he was also working up to his conclusion:

Now, provided you have not given me up as someone who is simply behind the times, but ask me more insistently than before what should be done with the Ten Commandments, I shall reply: Do what I am trying to do myself: to lead up to them. Not to a scroll, not even to the stone tablets on which 'the finger of God' (Exodus 31:18) once wrote the commandments, after they had been uttered; but to the Spoken Word.[22]

It is at such moments that attempts to introduce us to Martin Buber as a 'philosopher', or a 'religious philosopher', or even a 'religious existentialist philosopher', seem flatly beside the point. Why not simply say: the Jew?

*   *   *

There is something almost Shavian about the trenchant irony and vigorous salvationism of 'What Are We To Do About the Ten Commandments?' We must not conclude this chapter without trying to indicate how far the essence of the Mosaic element goes in Martin Buber and how hardly, but successfully, the Abrahamic element restores the balance. It is now sufficiently clear that Buber really feels to his roots his Judaism as the brotherhood of man. The antithesis is killing. The first fruit of Adam's heedless disobedience of the Spoken Word was the first killing, fratricide. The supreme commandment that inaugurated the second, Noachic, humanity was: 'Whoso sheddeth man's blood, by man shall his blood be shed; for in the image of God made He man.' The sixth commandment to Abrahamic man was, as the Masoretic text renders, 'Thou shalt not murder'. This makes the Book of Joshua disconcerting reading. The Chosen People enter the Holy Land with wholesale massacre of men, women and children, giving the authority of Moses for it.

Naturally, attempts have been made to square the circle. 'Murder' it is argued is a more restricted term than 'killing' and has to do with relations between man and man within Israelite society, not a limitation on the foreign policy that was unavoidable in a barbarous age, to say nothing of our own troubled times. Most modern nations take the same cue. One is suddenly reminded of a lethal satire by Osbert Sitwell, an early novel called *Miracle on Sinai*. It happens all over again, this time to a representative party of modern people staying at the luxury hotel which private enterprise has erected at the foot of this celebrated tourist attraction. This time too the tablets get broken to powder and down in the hotel again they begin to argue about what was on them. Each remembers only the commandment that most immediately concerns him, and remembers it in the form most convenient to himself. The great general Sir Rudyard Ramshackle, D.V.T.O., is emphatic that 'Sixth read: "Thou shalt do no murder; except when dressed in uniform, issued under the War Office Regulations." Makes things easier, doncherno!'

What is awkward about the convenient distinction between 'murder' and 'killing' is that it can hardly be read into the Noachic 'Whoso sheddeth man's blood . . .' The trouble with the enemy is that, indubitably, they bleed—as Shakespeare's heroine triumphantly reminded Shylock. Worse still, they cannot plausibly be excluded from 'for in the image of God made He man'. The distinction between 'murder' and 'killing' will also have to abrogate the brotherhood of man. Is it contended that the Mosaic formulation, the guidance for the third, Abrahamic, humanity, is in this vital respect more permissive than the direct Voice that spoke to the good, but not good enough, Noah?

But we are drifting into the pleasures of intellectual controversy on moral issues. We hasten back to living reality. In 1958, Buber spoke of the events in Palestine as the new State emerged. He had brought a storm upon his head at the time, and

long before, by advocating a bi-national State with the Arabs,
however difficult that might be to manage:

> How deep the evil had penetrated into a part of the people
> was first recognized by us when the fact could no longer be
> overlooked. Meanwhile, in opposition to the proposals for
> a binational state or a Jewish share in a Near East feder-
> ation, the unhappy partition of Palestine took place, the
> cleft between the two peoples was split asunder, the war
> raged. Everything proceeded with frightening logical con-
> sistency and at the same time with frightening meaning-
> lessness. It happened one day, however, that, outside of all
> regular conduct of the war, a band of armed Jews fell on an
> Arab village and destroyed it. Often in earlier times Arab
> hordes had committed outrages of this kind, and my soul
> bled with the sacrifice; but here it was a matter of our own,
> or my own crime, of the crime of Jews against the spirit.
> Even today I cannot think about this without feeling myself
> guilty. Our fighting faith in the spirit was too weak to
> prevent the outbreak and spread of false demonic teaching.[23]

But precisely this passionate championing of the sixth commandment is punctuated with a footnote, after the words 'the war
raged'.

> I must add here a personal remark because on this point I
> can speak for most, but not for all of my closest political
> friends. I am no radical pacifist; I do not believe that one
> must always answer violence with non-violence. I know
> what tragedy implies: when there is war, it must be fought.

Late in 1938, Gandhi recommended that the Jews in Germany
should use *Satyagraha*, non-violence, as the most effective reply to
Nazi atrocities. Buber appreciated the true stature of Gandhi and
that his spiritually motivated non-violent direct action was not
the same as the passive resistance or non-resistance advocated by
most Western Christian pacifists. He composed his answer slowly,
with many pauses. It was searing:

> Jews are being persecuted, robbed, maltreated, tortured,
> murdered. And you, Mahatma Gandhi, say that their
> position in the country where they suffer all this is an exact

parallel to the position of Indians in South Africa at the
time when you inaugurated your famous 'Strength of Truth'
or 'Soul Force' (*satyagraha*) campaign ... Now, do you
know or *do you not know*, Mahatma, what a concentration
camp is like and what goes on there? Do you know of the
torments in the concentration camp, of its methods of slow
and quick slaughter? I cannot assume that you know this ...
There is a certain situation in which from the '*satyagraha*'
of the strength of the spirit no '*satyagraha*' of the power of
truth can result. '*Satyagraha*' means testimony. Testimony
without acknowledgment, ineffective, unobserved martyrdom, a martyrdom cast to the winds—that is the fate of
innumerable Jews in Germany. God alone accepts their
testimony, and God 'seals' it, as is said in our prayers. But
no maxim for suitable behaviour can be deduced there-
from.[24]

We may be sure that Martin Buber did not condemn the
heroes of the last stand in the Warsaw Ghetto. We do not know
how Gandhi himself received this burning rebuke, but it is
recorded that he later described the Polish armed resistance to
the Nazi invasion as 'almost non-violent'—referring, of course,
to the spirit of it which so far transcended its resort to violence. It
may not be irrelevant to the purpose of this book, whose whole
intention is to commend the teaching of Martin Buber, to mention that its writer, a Gandhian pacifist at that time, renounced
dogmatic pacifism when he read Buber's letter to Gandhi, some
years after World War II.

But the relevant point here is that Buber does not bend, or
limit, or evade the Commandment. He accepts it as a supreme
human formulation of God's will that means what it says in the
full context of the divine image of man and human brotherhood.
But that image can be so fouled, that brotherhood so utterly
negated, that even the most absolute of the commandments of
how man should live with man must be—reverently and tragically—set aside. The figure of Abraham rises beside the figure of
Moses the Lawgiver. He accepted that it *was* the voice of God
that asked if he—like the idol-worshippers who sacrificed their
firstborn—would kill his beloved son, in whom was embodied
the whole promised future of Israel, the nation that was to be a

blessing to mankind and the earth. Isaac was spared; but not by Abraham, his own father. Buber writes on this in an essay in *Eclipse of God*. There he utters his most emphatic warning against mistaking mere political patriotism, or private passion, for pretext to set aside the Law:

> False absolutes rule over the soul, which is no longer able to put them to flight through the image of the true. Everywhere, over the whole surface of the human world—in the East and in the West, from the left and from the right, they pierce unhindered through the level of the ethical and demand of you 'the sacrifice'. Time and again, when I ask well-conditioned young souls, 'Why do you give up your dearest possession, your personal integrity?' they answer me, 'Even this, this most difficult sacrifice, is the thing that is needed in order that. . .' It makes no difference, 'in order that equality may come' or 'in order that freedom may come', it makes no difference! And they bring the sacrifice faithfully. In the realm of Moloch honest men lie and compassionate men torture. And they really and truly believe that brother-murder will prepare the way for brotherhood! There appears to be no escape from the most evil of all idolatry.[25]

That is presented here as the voice of the Mosaic element in Martin Buber. It is preceded by the Abrahamic:

> Abraham, to be sure, could not confuse with another the voice which once bade him leave his homeland and which he at that time recognized as the voice of God without the speaker saying to him who he was. And God did indeed 'tempt' him. Through the extremest demand He drew forth the innermost readiness to sacrifice out of the depths of Abraham's being, and He allowed this readiness to grow to full intention to act. He thus made it possible for Abraham's relation to Him, God, to become wholly real. But then, when no further hindrance stood between the intention and the deed, He contented Himself with Abraham's fulfilled readiness and prevented the action.[26]

If one could depend on prevention, the readiness would remain a theatrical gesture. But the Abrahamic is also theMosaic. It is the very root of the Decalogue that stands unshaken in the soul's and the world's long nightmare:

> I am the LORD thy God, who brought thee out of the land of Egypt, out of the house of bondage.
> Thou shalt have no other gods before Me.[27]

Perhaps we can now begin to understand why Martin Buber wrote, in *I and Thou*: 'This life may have fulfilled the law or broken it; both are continually necessary, that spirit may not die on earth.'

5

THE END OF THE WAY OF MAN: PSALMIST

W E have quoted the wise definition of Buber's attitude to
strict religious observance as metanomianism, the law of
the spirit. We have seen that for him the correspondence
of 'inner' and 'outer' is not a commonplace of the religious life,
or rather that it should be a commonplace so transfigured by
Abrahamic and Mosaic awareness that it becomes the central
reality of living. But if we are to feel something of the power,
intensity and persistence of Buber's understanding of the 'inner'
we must apprehend it in terms of his rendering of the Divine
Name: I WILL BE PRESENT AS EVER I WILL BE PRESENT. The
inner life is founded on the presence of God in every here and
now and on the ceaseless effort to apprehend that presence in its
always strictly unpredictable and unique manifestation. Provided that we have now clearly understood Buber's fundamental
distinction between 'unitive' mysticism, in which the human
personality claims to be merged with the Divine—a claim which
opens the door to the concept of the God-man that is central to
institutional Christianity—and 'dialogic' mysticism, in which the
closeness of relation is absolutely dependent upon the 'distance'
that necessarily separates the creature from the Creator, we may
understand this experience of the 'inner' life as mysticism:
Jewish mysticism. *Jewish Mysticism* was the title given by Lucy
Cohen to the translation of some of Buber's early Hasidic writings
which was the first volume of his work to appear in English.

Mysticism has been something of a problem in more than one
'organized' religion, if only for the simple reason that the
majority of its adherents and even of its ministers have found this
other than or beyond their own personal experience. Buber
would not, if we understand him correctly, accept the contention
that mysticism is for the few only, though he would doubtless
agree that the capacity is more or less developed in different
individuals. But the difference between the prophet—who has not
only his innate capacity but his calling—and you or I he would

perhaps hold to be ultimately one of degree and not of kind. Moses was asking much, when he exclaimed (Numbers 11:29) 'would that all the LORD's people were prophets, that the LORD would put his spirit upon them'. He was not asking the impossible.

In this, it will be said, Buber is at his most Hasidic. He might maintain that Hasidism is here at its most truly Biblical. But a distinction between Buber's mystical view of prayer and that of many other Jewish religious authorities must not be minimized if this portrait of the man is to have anything of his—not seldom controversial—individuality. The difference must not be exaggerated either. There is, of course, what Max Kadushin, in his valuable study of *The Rabbinic Mind* (1952) calls 'Normal Mysticism'. 'From almost every page of the rabbinic texts it is evident that the Rabbis *experienced* God, and that this experience was profound and unique' (p. 194). 'The ordinary, familiar, everyday things and occurrences, we have observed, constitute occasions for the experience of God' (p. 203). 'This means that every man, in the course of his everyday activities, has some experience of God . . . Of course, individuals who are particularly sensitive, or who possess other advantages of temperament, will apprehend more than those who are less gifted or perhaps less well-trained . . . In this kind of mysticism, the ordinary man closely approaches the gifted man' (p. 204). This should be sufficient to dispel any mistaken notions of a difference in *kind* between Rabbinic Judaism and Buber's dialogic mysticism, which is also very much a mysticism of the everyday and for everyman.

Still, the learned English Rabbi, Dr. Louis Jacobs, for instance, has been known to assert that he is no mystic, though he has done more than anyone in England to shed light on Hasidic mysticism, notably in his translation and brilliant elucidation of Dobh Baer's *Tract on Ecstasy*.[2] And in his short book, *Jewish Prayer*,[2] he does seem to intimate a clear distinction. The section on 'Types of Prayer' begins:

> There is more than one type of prayer. The earliest prayers were those of petition . . . There are, in addition, higher forms of prayer—the prayer of *thanksgiving* for favours received; the *penitential* prayer, asking God for forgiveness of

sins; and the *doxology*, the prayer of praise . . . all the types of prayer are found in the Prayer Book.[3]

But this is immediately preceded by a quotation from a letter written by Shneor Zalman, the Hasidic leader of whom was related, in our first chapter, the story of his encounter with the police chief:

> . . . the idea of prayer and its essence is the foundation of the whole Torah. Namely to know God . . .[4]

This separation draws attention to the fact that the 'types of prayer' specified do not presume to speak of 'knowing' God; they define various human attitudes and are silent, however devoutly, as to the response. They do not describe prayer as essentially a *dialogue*. And, on the other hand, the Hasidic leader's bold definition—'namely, to *know* God'—which has not been brought under the heading 'types of prayer'—focuses attention on 'to *know*' in something like the full intensity of the Biblical use of that word to indicate the most full and intimate of meetings, though not one from which the 'mystery' is lifted.

Thus alerted by the fairness and discrimination of Dr. Jacobs' treatment of Jewish prayer, we shall no longer be surprised at— or tempted to dismiss as of no great significance—the fact that while almost exactly half the one hundred and fifty Psalms are included in the Authorized Daily Prayer Book, the Psalm that is most prominent and precious in the writings of Martin Buber is not among them. (Although, to be precise, verses 25–26 of Psalm 73 are merged in the 'Home Service Prior to Funeral'—27th ed., 1961, pp. 317a–b.)

*   *   *

In Nahum Glatzer's *Franz Rosenzweig: His Life and Thought*,[5] we read how, after continuing his labours with Martin Buber on the translation of the Hebrew Bible, under the worst of afflictions, Rosenzweig died towards the end of 1929 and was buried on 12th December in the new cemetery of the Jewish community:

> In accordance with Franz Rosenzweig's wish, there was no funeral oration. Martin Buber read Psalm 73, which contains the inscription Franz Rosenzweig chose for his headstone.[6]

Seven years later, when Buber had been forbidden to speak to his fellow Jews by the Nazi authorities, he used the method known as 'the new Midrash' to deliver his message, his purposeful selection of twenty-three Psalms, *Out of the depths have I cried unto Thee*. Psalm 73 is the thirteenth in that series. It would be beyond the scope of this book and foreign to the genius of Martin Buber to attempt to discover recondite meanings here by a sort of pseudo-Kabbalistic numerology. But numbers are often used in the Bible itself to allude—in a manner that may be inadequately called 'poetic'—to basic elements in the Biblical pattern. Thus, if we know—as it will at once appear that we do—that Psalm 73 is specially sacred to Martin Buber, we can scarcely fail to reflect that its thirteenth position mirrors the transfiguration of the twelve Abrahamic tribes into what we have already styled the thirteenth entity, the holy nation, Israel; and that the ten following Psalms suggest the Ten Commandments that are, so to say, the essential Mosaic constitution of that people of priests. Psalm 73—it would perhaps be to consider too curiously to record the first associations to these digits, separately and together—is thus, in this series, the 'and' that separates and relates the 'I' and 'Thou' of the Abrahamic and the Mosaic.

More than a decade later, the War and the holocaust over and the new Israel just emerging in troubled birth, Buber devoted several pages of *The Prophetic Faith* to the seventy-third Psalm, in which he defines its unique significance to him:

It is 'a message of God to the whole of mankind together'. At the basis of such prophetic prayer, meant to be the expression and transmission of a revelation, there lies hid an overwhelming experience of life, the novelty and strength of which act upon the recipient as a mission. This is not felt so strongly in any other Psalm as in Psalm 73, of which it has rightly been said that that actual experience had almost entirely dissolved the old fixed style and created a special form. The motive in the creation of this form is that it is necessary to make known the most personal matter, to lay bare the secret of the heart, in order that the manifestation be really effected. It is not permissible to translate it from the intimate language of prayer into a more objective manner of speech: the one who prays cannot perform his

testimony without preserving the immediacy of the relationship between the 'I' and the 'thou'. The fact that the prophetic meaning of his prayer, its message meaning, is
perceived by him, turns it into a confession.[7]

This apprehension of the 'prophetic' character of Psalm 73 is
further unfolded in the small book on five Psalms, *Right and
Wrong*, that soon followed—in which the seventy-third Psalm
occupies the climactic fourth place, followed only by Psalm One
(in which we may not be wrong to read the allusion to the One
God and the always necessary new beginning).

> It is a revelation. It would be a misunderstanding of the
> whole situation to look on this as a pious feeling. From
> man's side there is no continuity, only from God's side. The
> Psalmist has learned that God and he are continually with
> one another. But he cannot express his experience as a word
> of God. The teller of the primitive stories made God say to
> the fathers and to the first leaders of the people: 'I am with
> thee', and the word 'continually' was unmistakably heard
> as well. Thereafter, this was no longer reported and we hear
> it again only in rare prophecies. A Psalmist (23:5) is still
> able to say of God: 'Thou art with me.' But when Job
> (29:5) speaks of God's having been with him in his youth,
> the fundamental word, the 'continually', has disappeared.
> The speaker in our Psalm is the first and only one to insert
> it expressly. He no longer says: 'Thou art with me', but 'I
> am continually with thee'. It is not, however, from his own
> consciousness and feeling that he can say this, for no man is
> able to be continuously turned to the presence of God: he
> can say it only in the strength of the revelation that God is
> continually with him.

* * *

What the Psalmist of Psalm 73 reveals from the innermost depths
of his own personal experience is what we have tried to indicate
by calling this chapter 'The End of the Way of Man'. The phrase
is intentionally twofold. By 'the end of the way' we may mean the
objective, the goal of life. Or, equally, we may mean by it 'the
end' in the sense of the end of one man's life. According to Martin
Buber, Psalm 73 does indeed deal in both these meanings, and in

his view—which most of his commentators do not discuss—its answer is fundamentally the same in both cases. The goal of the prayerful life, we have just seen, is the full realization—not merely a doctrinal 'belief that'—that 'I am continually with thee', although in all but the most rare and precious moments the speaker is unaware of the Presence. How could the goal in death be otherwise? Even if there is no 'survival' in the prose sense, no conscious continuity in which the Presence is known, the speaker knows *now* that the Presence, which is eternal, will persist and insofar as it has really been the light of his life, has given him existence as against the virtual 'nothingness', the non-existence, of the denier of God, it can be truly said that he is continually, and for always, with God.

This position, that 'life' can be 'non-existence' and death a persistence in the presence of the Eternal is so strange—if not, to many, unacceptable—that a warning seems necessary here. We are mainly concerned in this book to indicate what are Martin Buber's principal Biblical interpretations, and how his understanding of Hasidism and his own modern 'philosophy' conform to them. It is to be hoped that no responsible reader will base a judgment of those interpretations on what is here presented as an outline of them, without studying the testimony and expositions, stemming from Buber's own experience rather than from discursive thinking, in the originals, to which he is commended. But to dispel the possible reaction that in denying 'survival' Buber finally cuts himself off from authentic Judaism, we may here mention the verdict of Yehezkel Kaufman, in his monumental study of *The Religion of Israel*:

> The realm of the dead, the rites connected with death and burial, as well as the destiny of the soul in the other world, play no part in the religion of YHVH. This is one of the most astonishing features of Israelite religion. That the spirit of the deceased lives on apart from the body is the belief of the people, but biblical faith draws no religious or moral inferences from this notion.[9]

We may now glance briefly at the language in which Buber presents his insights on the teaching of Psalm 73 about 'the end of the way of man'. There is no system of divine material reward and punishment:

God does not requite the evil man, there is no reckoning between God and man, but to be without God means not to be.[10]

Here, if possible with even greater emphasis, is the distinction between the fate of the wayfarer and that of the wanderer that we presented in the first chapter. And again Buber stresses, in even fewer and so more highly charged words:

> Sin is not the cause of death but death itself.[11]

If such statements strike us as exaggerated or merely metaphorical that is because we have not followed the way of the master of prayer who uttered the seventy-third Psalm. It was not enough that he 'purified his heart', though that is no light matter:

> Even when he succeeded in being able 'to wash his hands in innocence' (which does not mean an action or feeling of self-righteousness, but the genuine, second and higher purity which is won by a great struggle of the soul), the torment continued . . .[12]

—until he 'came into the sanctuaries of God'. And although, as Buber does not mention, Psalm 73 is 'A Psalm of Asaph', and there is a wonderful evocation in the Bible (2 Chronicles 5) of Solomon's dedication of the Temple, with Asaph (v. 12) as first singer—

> This does not mean the temple precincts in Jerusalem, but the sphere of God's holiness, the holy mysteries of God. Only to him who draws near to these is the true meaning of the conflict revealed.[13]

This true meaning, as we have already indicated, is not

> that the present state of affairs is replaced by a future state of affairs of a quite different kind, in which 'in the end' things go well with the good and badly with the bad, in the language of modern thought the meaning is that the bad do not truly exist, and their 'end' brings about only this change, that they now inescapably experience their non-existence, the suspicion of which they had again and again succeeded in dispelling.[14]

They have not, in the elemental language of Buber's own modern formulation, attained the 'I' that comes into existence only in the act of truly saying 'Thou'.

*   *   *

Theology certainly maintains that God is immanent as well as transcendent, but it is noticeable that many religious people proceed on the unexamined assumption that Heaven and Earth are spatially remote realms of reality, that God is to be imagined in the former—directing terrestial affairs, perhaps, by some kind of mysterious remote control, but otherwise only a very occasional visitor, manifest to the select few. They do not, for instance, speak as though they are convinced that Heaven is wherever God is and that, since God is in some sense eternal and infinite, that necessarily means—in every here and now. So there is something almost sensational to many readers in Buber's comment on the cry in Psalm 73, 'Whom have I in heaven?'—

> he does not turn his eyes away from the sufferings of earth, persistent as they are, he does not turn to the delights of heaven, it is not heaven with which he is concerned, but *God*, Who is no more in heaven than in earth, but is near him; he does not long to be in heaven, but where he is with God, and if he is with Him, there is nothing on earth which he could desire (v. 25).[15]

And this leads on, without pause, to the meaning of death and the myth—in the true sense of Biblical myth that we have sought to establish as central to Buber's total life-experience as an Abrahamic man—of 'survival':

> If his flesh and with it his heart will fail, this heart which formerly effervesced and now experiences the nearness of God, He, Who lives in this perishable heart as the imperishable 'rock' and became his 'portion' (v. 26) remains forever, and this is enough. Lasting is of God: he lasts who is near to God . . .[16]

In case the phrase 'He, who lives in this perishable heart' suggests something like the exclusively subjective 'divinity' of Kant, we must at once add the complementary assertion from Buber's other main exposition of Psalm 73:

Only the 'rock' in which the heart is concealed, only the rock of human hearts does not vanish. For it does not stand in time. The time of the world disappears before eternity, but existing man dies into eternity as into the perfect existence.[17]

Buber does not believe that this ultimate insight of the Psalmist is in any way at odds with the total context of the Hebrew Bible. The Psalmist:

does not mean that he will be taken up to heaven, but he believes that God will care for him in death as in life, that He will be actively present to him also in death. Beyond this certainty that God does not remove his presence from His saints even in death, the Psalmist does not allow his imagination to play. It is indeed true, in my opinion, that the belief in enduring bliss 'did not take root in Judaism until a later age and not without the influence of foreign religions' if by the word 'belief' we mean here an orderly religious world view. But there are in Israel, as in other peoples, primordial forms of belief in the power God's nearness exercises over death. Indeed, men leave these forms of the belief—and apparently intentionally—in the mystery of the mythical element, until they are recast in the fire of new and strong experiences of communion with God. The decisive fact is that the conception of God becomes more real and more powerful than that of death: men put their 'refuge' in YHVH (Psalm 73:28)—beyond this they do not go, and obviously this is real enough. It is not the 'immortality of the soul' that is the concern of this belief, but the eternity of God. It is not important what dying appears to be in the eyes of man: if he lives in communion with God, he knows that God is eternal and that He is his portion.[18]

As we read these words, we come to know, surely, something of what Martin Buber felt when he read Psalm 73 at the grave of Franz Rosenzweig.

*   *   *

We have already learned from another source that, for the Hasidic leader Shneor Zalman, to know God—that is, of course, to apprehend the presence of God, who is unknowable in Himself—is 'the idea' of prayer and the foundation of the whole Torah. One of Buber's *Tales of the Hasidim* goes so far as to insist that prayer is nothing else but this realization of the presence:

> At the close of the seventy-second Psalm are the words: 'And let the whole earth be filled with His glory. Amen and Amen. The prayers of David the son of Jesse are ended.'
>
> Concerning this Rabbi Levi Yitzhak said: 'All prayer and hymns are a plea to have His glory revealed throughout the world. But if once the whole is, indeed, filled with it, there will be no further need to pray.'[19]

It is perhaps significant that this position is here based on a reading of the end of Psalm 72. And whereas we quoted from two of Buber's works to bring together the complementary truths of the experience of God's immanence and transcendence—of God as the imperishable 'rock' in the heart, and of the 'rock' in which the heart is concealed—we find in his selection of Hasidic sayings, and in relation to Psalm 73, both aspects together. The sixth of the *Ten Rungs*, 'The Rung of the Way', concludes with the item, of which the title may be read in both senses, 'He Who Has a Heart':

> He who has a heart, is not concerned with space and place, for he himself is the place of the world. For God is in one's heart, as we read in the psalm: 'God is the rock of my heart.' And God speaks to Moses: 'Behold, there is a place by Me.' We know that God is the place of the world and that it is not the world which is his place. And the same holds for him who has a heart, since God is in his heart. He whose heart is the heart of Israel must not say: 'This place does not suit me,' for place and space cannot matter to him, because he is the place of the world, and the world is not his place.[20]

It is clear that this relates, not only outwardly in its direct quotation of Psalm 73, but inwardly to Buber's exposition of that Psalm in his Biblical writings, and that something beyond the pleasures of critical recognition is to be gained by the setting of them in right relation. To the general reader, as yet unaccustomed to the fully responsible solemnity with which Buber utters every word, the short Hasidic saying might be glanced over as little more than a rather involved bit of homiletics, lacking the undeniable 'literary' appeal of some of the Hasidic tales. The reader of *Ten Rungs* has been discreetly warned in its Preface, which concludes:

> I have selected, reduced to the quintessence of meaning, and arranged them according to major themes, not because they are beautiful and interesting, but because of my belief that, in this selection, arrangement and form, they may serve to show even the reader who is very remote from their origins the way to the true life.[21]

But we have at least the advantage of knowing that 'He Who Has a Heart' points to Psalm 73's disclosure of a long and arduous struggle for a state of realization that is not to be attained only by—nor indeed without—'purifying the heart', nor by—or without—'the washing of the hands in innocence' by which is signified a second and higher purity, won only by a great struggle of the soul, but only by the attainment called 'coming into the sanctuaries of God': there—in the here and now of any and every time and place in which this full maturity of the Abrahamic consciousness is attained and vouchsafed—the Presence is apprehended: and no more can be required. Here, perhaps, the method adopted in this book must be judged. Either what Buber presents on Psalm 73 in his Hasidic writings is illuminated by what he says about that Psalm in his directly Biblical writings—or it is not. But it is, anyway, only the extreme instance of the relationship between different 'strata' of his work that we have been concerned to trace, and of which it is our contention—which should be, but has not been, self-evident—that the Biblical is the bed-rock.

The life of prayer, conceived as the unending pursuit of the Presence of the One God whose name Moses rendered I WILL BE PRESENT AS EVER I WILL BE PRESENT, is not at all without its perils. The main ones, on which Buber dwells, and from which he maintains that essential Hasidism liberated the earlier Kabbalism, are the temptations of gnosis and magic. In gnosis, the abuse is the endeavour to pierce the veils of the mystery of the divine Presence, in magic to find means to conjure and constrain the Presence. But Psalm 73 is used, once more, by Buber in *Tales of the Hasidim* to warn against a temptation or at least a misunderstanding that may have not a little to do with the brisk sales of many popular and other works on 'mysticism'. This is, of course, the fallacy that the object of the exercise is self-improvement. How pleasant for oneself, how gratifying that one's acquaintance can hardly fail to notice how enlightened one has become, in what exalted spiritual society one now moves. Into this agreeable fantasy the reckless word of a Hasidic rabbi breaks with the irresistible voice of reality:

> Once when Rabbi Mordecai (of Lekhovitz) was saying the verse from the Psalm: 'But I was brutish and ignorant; I was as a beast before Thee,' he interrupted himself and cried: 'Lord of the world, I want to be ignorant, I want to be brutish, if only I can be before Thee.'[22]

*   *   *

Rabbi Nachman, the great-grandson of the Baal Shem Tov, told longer symbolic stories, more elaborate than the Hasidic legends of the *Tales of the Hasidim*. Martin Buber's renovations of the versions of a few of them that had been imperfectly transmitted was the first-fruit of his five years' study of Hasidism, and he has told us that it was with the last two of the half-dozen *Tales of Rabbi Nachman* (1906) that he felt himself in full rapport with the rabbi. The fifth story, of which nothing can be detached for separate citation here, is 'The Master of Prayer'.

That Nachman was himself a 'master' of prayer, Buber goes far to persuade us in his account, already quoted (it is to be found both in *Israel and Palestine* and appended to the 1956 and 1962 editions of *The Tales of Rabbi Nachman*, and is indeed to be read together with them) of Nachman's inner and outer journey to Palestine, where there are enigmatic hints—no others are possible in the nature of the case—of the perils of the soul. We have already mentioned his preliminary night in the Jewless city of Kamieniec. We return to it for a moment here because its outcome is suggested in a quotation from another Psalm, which indicates that Nachman had indeed reached the goal of prayer:

> On his return home he delivers an exposition on the Psalm verse: 'My soul has clung unto Thee, Thy right hand has held me up.' (Psalm 63:9)[23]

This line may also have been in Buber's mind when he wrote of the Psalmist of Psalm 73's 'Thou holdest my right hand':

> The Psalmist no longer dares to express the central experience as a word of God; but he expressed it by a gesture of God. God has taken his right hand—as a father, so we may add, in harmony with that expression 'the generation of thy children', takes his little son by the hand in order to lead him. More precisely, as in the dark a father takes his little son by the hand, certainly in order to lead him, but primarily in order to make present to him, in the warm touch of coursing blood, the fact that he, the father, is continually with him.[24]

But to return to Rabbi Nachman's own exposition of the text from Psalm 63:

> The exposition has not come down to us, but we can guess the gist of it: He to whom his soul has clung from his childhood days—we know of the boy's tempestuous search for the favour of God—has now stretched forth his hand to support him.[25]

There follows a sentence which many may find unacceptable, superstitious, or even bordering on the blasphemous, since there is always a temptation to reduce God to a manageable 'father-figure' and to omit, or exonerate Him from, for instance, any kind of responsibility for an untimely death. Yet, if we find mythic significance in, for instance, the various fates of the several offspring of Adam, Noah and Abraham, the 'fathers' of the three 'races' of mankind, we shall at least come near to beginning to understand how Rabbi Nachman received what happened next:

> But at the same time his little daughter dies, and he connects this too with the new process that has begun; this too is strictly part of the context of the simultaneously wholly factual and wholly symbolical proceedings.
>
> On the even of the Feast of the Passover he says, coming out of the ritual plunge-bath, to his attendant: 'In this year I shall certainly be in the Holy Land.' The speech which he makes on the Feast is based on the Psalm verse: 'Thy way is

in the sea, and thy path in the great waters and thy foot-steps are not known.' (Psalm 77:19)[26]

Psalm 77, like Psalm 73, is 'A Psalm of Asaph'.

We must add an inadequate word on the Hasidic view of death and 'survival'. It cannot be simply equated with Buber's mature reading—it is one of the very few vital questions on which he came to revise his earlier position—of the teaching of Psalm 73 on 'survival'. In however mythical a way, the Hasidim seem to have believed—and here they were probably far from the main Hebrew tradition—in some sort of transmigration of souls and in reincarnation. (Of the mystery of the personal and corporate identity of the suffering Servant, and of that succession, we shall say something in the final chapter.) Consequently, there was no obstacle to their expressing their still living veneration of past zaddiks in impressions of their progress beyond death. What concerns us here is that even this was not conceived as a union with God. The way towards God was a way without end because its goal was infinite. In what may be judged the most openly eloquent of all Buber's early writing, the famous essay on 'The Life of the Hasidim' in *The Legend of the Baal-Shem* (it is also included in the later volume, *Hasidism and Modern Man*), he wrote of *hitlahavut* (ecstasy):

> But *hitlahavut* is not a sudden sinking into eternity: it is an ascent to the infinite from rung to rung. To find God means to find the way without end. The Hasidim saw the 'world to come' in the image of this way, and they never called that world a Beyond. One of the pious saw a dead master in a dream. The latter told him that from the hour of his death he went each day from world to world. And the world which yesterday was stretched out above his gaze as heaven is today the earth under his foot; and the heaven of today is the earth of tomorrow. And each world is purer and more beautiful and more profound than the one before.[27]

This may have more appeal to some than Buber's contention that the Hebrew Bible has no teaching of 'enduring bliss'. But to him, at least, nothing could be more pure, more beautiful and more profound than that 'the conception of God becomes more real and more powerful than that of death', that 'It is not im-portant what dying appears to be in the eyes of man: if he lives in communion with God, he knows that God is eternal and that He is his portion.'

* * *

We turn once more to Martin Buber the modern 'philosopher', who has been helpfully advised to liberate his teachings from their 'confessional limitations' and whose 'philosophy of dialogue' has been reduced to little more than a cliché by specialists eager to 'apply' these 'theoretical' positions in their own field of psychiatric or pedagogic or other work. What Buber has said, and said so well, is certainly useful in many fields. Only (some of his professed admirers seem privately to reflect at times), how odd of God to choose the Jew.

There is small excuse for the non-religious 'thinker' who may thus think to skim the comradely cream from Buber's 'philosophy' and in fact only misses the real riches. In *I and Thou*, in which I think the word 'Jew' occurs only once—in the context of birth— he not only writes that 'two great servants pace through the ages, prayer and sacrifice'[28] but virtually identifies religion with prayer in words that irresistibly recall those of Shneor Zalman that were quoted at the beginning of this chapter:

> In true prayer belief and cult are united and purified to enter into the living relation. The fact that true prayer lives in the religions witnesses to their true life: they live so long as it lives in them. Degeneration of the religions means degeneration of prayer in them.[29]

And it is in the book in which Buber considers the modern philosophers that the basic distinction is made in its most uncompromising form. *Eclipse of God*, he writes,

> discusses the relations between religion and philosophy in the history of the spirit and deals with the part that philosophy has played in its late period in making God and all absoluteness appear unreal.[30]

But the religion that is here contrasted with philosophy may survive within, but must by no means be simply identified with, religion as dogma, law, concept and ritual, with what seems to be the almost inescapable systematization of institutional religion:

If philosophy is here set in contrast to religion, what is meant by religion is not the massive fulness of statements, concepts and activities that one customarily describes by this name and that men sometimes long for more than for God. Religion is essentially the act of holding fast to God. And that does not mean holding fast to an image that one has made of God, nor even holding fast to the faith in God that one has conceived. It means holding fast to the existing God. The earth would not hold fast to its conception of the sun (if it had one) nor to its connection with it, but to the sun itself. [31]

And here, in this book in which Buber confronts some typical modern philosophers, after specific warning against the opposite dangers of gnosis and magic, of 'unveiling' and 'conjuring' (which are practices by no means confined to ambitious Kabbalists), he defines true prayer and the self-division that makes prayer almost impossible to modern man, which brings about the eclipse of the God who is hidden only by the shadow we interpose.

We call prayer in the pregnant sense of the term that speech of Man to God which, whatever else is asked, ultimately asks for the manifestation of the divine Presence, for this Presence's becoming dialogically perceivable. The single presupposition of a genuine state of prayer is thus the readiness of the whole man for this Presence, simple turned-towardness, unreserved spontaneity. This spontaneity, ascending from the roots, succeeds time and again in overcoming all that disturbs and diverts. But in this our stage of subjectivized reflection not only the concentration of the one who prays, but also his spontaneity is assailed. The assailant is consciousness, the over-consciousness of this man here that he is praying, that he is *praying*, that *he* is praying. And the assailant appears to be invincible. The subjective knowledge of the one turning-towards about his turning-towards, this holding back of an I which does not enter into the action with the rest of the person, an I to which the action is an object—all this depossesses the moment, takes away its spontaneity. The specifically modern man who has not yet let go of God knows what this means: he who is not present perceives no Presence.[32]

There is in this essay on 'God and the Spirit of Man' no overt reference to Psalm 73. But its presence, the presence of what it conveys to Martin Buber, breathes in every word of the passage just quoted.

* * *

The fundamental question remains, or at least the implied answer to it has yet to be made as explicit as is possible in the nature of the case. That in prayer, which is to say in all right living, we should seek the Presence, all may agree 'in principle'. That the Presence has been realized in some degree by exceptional men the Bible testifies in a manner that carries its own immediate conviction to the reader—even the modern reader—who is genuinely open to it. Abraham's dialogue with God over the destruction of Sodom *is* dialogue. Moses' interrogation of God at the burning bush is answered by a revelation that cannot be limited within—as it also cannot be imagined without—the working of his own 'conscience' at having left his people in slavery to a foreign master. And we have yet to consider the later prophets, with their distinguishing 'saith the Lord'.

But how can man, the ordinary Adam, the average decent Noachic man of goodwill, or even the rank and file son of the Abrahamic covenant, aspire—without intolerable and perhaps disastrous presumption—to such Mosaic heights? And should he do so, will he not fall victim to self-delusion, to schizophrenic fantasies of receiving some infinitely rarefied Third Programme of enlightened guidance, comprehensible only to a spiritual cognoscenti to which he has been not so much elected as self-appointed? We have been told what is the essential posture and purpose of prayer. But what *is* the reply, the response that entitles us to use, with all its overwhelming implications, the fateful word—dialogue?

In 'Dialogue', the essay which opens *Between Man and Man*, the volume which develops the implications of *I and Thou*, there is a short section on 'The Signs'. There are probably many modern psychiatrists who would be much perturbed by it as exemplary teaching, although there are doubtless also those who do not suppose that they, any more than the rest of us, have been vouch-safed full knowledge of ultimate realities, and who will therefore remain open to a serious consideration of what is here taught. 'The Signs' begins with a warning that reminds us of the 'hide-outs' that every Adam employs, as though by second nature, to escape God's constant question, 'Where art thou?'

> Each of us is encased in an armour whose task is to ward off signs. Signs happen to us without respite, living means being addressed, we would need only to present ourselves and to perceive. But the risk is too dangerous for us, the soundless thunderings seem to threaten us with annihilation, and from generation to generation we perfect the defence apparatus. All our knowledge assures us: 'Be calm, every-thing happens as it must happen, but nothing is directed at you, you are not meant; it is just 'the world', you can ex-perience it as you like, but whatever you make of it in your-self proceeds from you alone, nothing is required of you, you are not addressed, all is quiet.'[33]

Still, if 'signs happen to us without respite', and if we go out with our whole being to meet them so that, like the lovestruck knight in Giraudoux's *Ondine*, all our armour falls off at the spirit's lightest 'word', we still expect that they will be disclosed as something highly extraordinary, angelic visions perhaps or a voice pronouncing words of revelation or commandment? (Perhaps voices and visions are true myths of intense experience of 'the signs' by exceptional persons?) But:

> The signs of address are not something extraordinary, something that steps out of the order of things, they are just what goes on time and again, just what goes on in any case, nothing is added by the address. The waves of the aether roar on always, but for most of the time we have turned off our receivers.

> What occurs to me addresses me. In what occurs to me the world happening addresses me.[33]

Buber is aware that this will be taken by some of the 'door-keepers' of the 'tower of the ages'—we are reminded of the Tower of Babel that was to reach heaven—as 'a variety of primitive superstition', since by the address of the world-happening to each and every person he clearly does not mean anything that can be rationally reduced to the categories (in themselves genuinely admirable) of physics, biology and sociology—the domains, we may remark, of those influential secularized Jewish prophets, Einstein, Freud and Marx. But he also separates himself from the augurs 'of whom, as is well known, there are remarkable modern varieties—

> But whether they haruspicate or cast a horoscope their signs have this peculiarity that they are in a dictionary, even if not necessarily a written one. It does not matter how esoteric the information that is handed down: he who searches out the signs is *well up in* what life's juncture this or that sign means ... This is not even the aping of a real faith.
>
> Real faith—if I may so term presenting ourselves and perceiving—begins when the dictionary is put down, when you are done with it. What occurs to me says something to me, but what it says to me cannot be revealed by any esoteric information; for it has never been said before nor is it composed of sounds that have ever been said. It can neither be interpreted nor translated, I can have it neither explained nor displayed; it is not a *what* at all, it is said into my very life; it is no experience that can be remembered independently of the situation, it remains the address of that moment and cannot be isolated, it remains the question of a questioner and will have its answer.[35]

The section of 'Dialogue' called 'The Signs'—it has been hard to abstain from simply quoting it verbatim—concludes with the key word. We experience the everyday, the commonplace, the here and now, as the address to each of us by the Presence when we know that both it and ourselves are the creation of the Creator who has neither died, as Nietzsche put it, nor retired to concern himself with matters doubtless more momentous, but is its—and our—constantly sustaining Presence, if we condescend to notice it.

The true name of concrete reality is the creation which is

entrusted to me and to every man. In it the signs of address are given to us. [36]

*　　*　　*

In the Introduction we quoted from Martin Buber's essay, 'The Man of Today and the Jewish Bible' in *Israel and the World*. At one point, the Bible is defined in a single sentence:

> The Jewish Bible is the historical document of a world swinging between creation and redemption, which, in the course of its history, experiences revelation, a revelation which *I* experience *if I am there*. Thus, we can understand that the resistance of the man of today is that of his innermost being. [37]

In this chapter we have been concerned with prayer as the becoming present of the person who then becomes aware of the Presence. It is also called 'the turning'. Its only watchword is 'Begin again'. But since we are considering 'the end of the way of man' not only in the sense of this immediate and constant objective but in the related sense of the mystery of his 'end' in death itself, we may conclude with the words about redemption that close 'The Man of Today and the Jewish Bible':

> The lived moment leads directly to the knowledge of revelation, and thinking about birth leads indirectly to the knowledge of creation. But in his personal life probably not one of us will taste the essence of redemption before his last hour. And yet here too, there is an approach. It is dark and silent and cannot be indicated by any means, save by my asking you to recall your own dark and silent hours. I mean those hours in the lowest depths when our soul hovers over the frail trap door which, at the very next instant, may send us down into destruction, madness, and 'suicide' at our own verdict. Indeed, we are astonished that it has not opened up until now. But suddenly we feel a touch as of a hand. It reaches down to us, it wishes to be grasped—and yet what incredible courage is needed to take the hand, to let it draw us up out of the darkness! This is redemption. We must realize the true nature of the experience proferred us: It is that our 'redeemer liveth' (Job 19:18), that he wishes to

redeem us—but only by our own acceptance of his redemption with the turning of our whole being.

Approach, I said. For all this still does not constitute a rootedness in biblical reality. But it is the approach to it. It is a beginning.[38]

And in the phrasing of what comes to us when we are in 'the lowest depths', the touch of a hand that reaches down to us, we hear once more the accents of the writer of Psalm 73:

> Nevertheless I am continually with Thee;
> Thou holdest my right hand.

We have related how in 1929 Martin Buber read Psalm 73 at the funeral of Franz Rosenzweig whose headstone bore a quotation from it. Thirty-six years later the headstone of Buber's own grave in Jerusalem bore the same quotation as his friend's —in Hebrew, the first word is simply 'And':

> Nevertheless I am continually with Thee.

THE WAY OF THE WORLD: ISAIAH

ARTIN Buber sees the Biblical interpretation of history
as the antithesis of what is usually regarded as 'real
history'. What historians, mainly concerned with
decisive battles, power politics and other criteria of 'success',
present as meaningful history is not true history at all:

> ... what the Bible understands by history is a dialogue in
> which man, in which the people, is spoken to and fails to
> answer, yet where the people in the midst of its failure
> continually rises up and tries to answer. It is the history of
> God's disappointments, but this history of disappointments
> constitutes a way that leads from disappointment to dis-
> appointment and beyond all disappointments; it is the way
> of the people, the way of man, yes, the way of God through
> mankind.[1]

Under the kingship of God, through the Law revealed to all at
Sinai, there need have been no such disappointments. Responsibility rests on each and all of the people of priests. Had the first
generations of the chosen people responded unanimously the
ideal human community might actually have come into full
existence in their time and its example would have spread like
wildfire among the perplexed nations until, as Israel itself had
become a great family of families, the world would have been a
community of communities.

But humanity cannot dispense with human leadership. It
needed Moses to lead out the people (as God had led out the first
of them, Abraham) and Moses to lead them after the revelation
at Sinai. Whatever the failings of Moses, they were as nothing to
the failures among his multitude of followers. This is the perennial
tragedy of leadership. A people will concede greater responsibility to its leaders only so that it may enjoy less responsibility
itself. If Moses converses with God, it saves them the exertion of
doing so themselves. If they undertake to follow, to obey, their
accepted leaders in some matters and in certain critical circum-

stances, it is on the understanding that over a great area of life they may go their own ways most of the time—and as their ways amount to abandonment of dedicated wholeness to the bidding and domination of impulses now grown autonomous, these are in fact no ways, each man's true 'I' is lost in its own disintegration and the true 'We' does not come into being.

In *The Prophetic Faith*, Buber outlines the Biblical history of Israel from some such standpoint as this, a view that will no doubt be more fully available to English readers when the forthcoming translation of *Konigtum Gottes* (*Kingship of God*), the promised volume on Samuel (of which one section has appeared in Hebrew) and the English version of the Mystery Play *Elijah* are published.[2] The 'leave it to the leaders' attitude fails in ways which history fully dramatizes. The era of leaders personally adopted for specific tasks and limited durations—the Judges— issues in the loss of the Ark itself to Israel's enemies. The false conclusion is drawn. This failure is due, it is said, not to the people's own shortcomings, which frustrate the emergence of the holy nation, but to its lack of what other nations have—a divinely guaranteed hereditary leadership in the form of a monarchic dynasty. This is reluctantly granted to them and results in an aggravation of the separation of sacred and secular spheres, which history again dramatizes in the calamity of two kings and two warring kingdoms, a divided nation doomed to fall.

> But now in the situation of the failure of kings the new and last type of leader in biblical history arises, the leader who above all other types is 'contrary to history', the Prophet, he who is appointed to oppose the king, and even more, history.[3]

The prophet is not the reversal of the failure of leadership but its climax. The existence of the long line of prophets—

> is failure through and through. They live in failure; it is for them to fight and not to conquer.[4]

Yet the Bible is adamant in its certitude. 'The history of God's disappointments' is the way that leads beyond all disappointments. It is precisely in the climactic disappointment of the rejection and suffering of the prophets that the pearl forms.

When the Bible then tries to look beyond these manifestations of leadership to one which no longer stands amidst
disintegration and failure, when the idea of the messianic
leader is conceived, it means nothing else by it than that at
last the answer shall be given: from out of mankind itself the
word shall come, the word that is spoken with the whole
being of man, the word that answers God's word. It is an
earthly consummation that is awaited, a consummation in
and with mankind. But this precisely is the consummation
toward which God's hand pushes, through nature and
through history. This is what the Messianic belief means, the
belief in the real leader, in the setting right of the dialogue,
in God's disappointment being at an end. [5]

The teaching of the Suffering Servant, of the Messiah, is a
phenomenon that seems, to Christians, to have been vindicated
some two thousand years ago. To the non-religious mind it may
seem as pathetically explicable as the dreams of sumptuous
banquets that sometimes visit starving men. In the final chapter,
we shall turn to Buber's view of it, and of the mysterious figure of
the 'second Isaiah'. Here we limit ourselves to Buber's understanding of the first Isaiah, the prophet 'appointed to oppose the
king, and even more, history'.

*   *   *

Buber's inaugural lecture at the Hebrew University in Jerusalem
in 1938 was on 'The Demand of the Spirit and Historical
Reality'. His contrast of Plato and Isaiah,[6] of philosophy and
religion, is significant. Philosophy has tended towards the assertion of human self-sufficiency. Religion relies on a spirit whose
true servant it strives to become. (More than a decade later,
Buber examined some typical modern manifestations of autarchic
philosophy in his book *Eclipse of God*.) Here we are concerned
with Buber's first words in Jerusalem about the prophet whose
dark way lies through failure that is foretold at the outset, but
who, by that very failure in the line of dedicated duty, is permitted to see beyond failure to the end of 'the way of the world'.

'In the year that King Uzziah died' (Isaiah 6:1) Isaiah had
a vision of the heavenly sanctuary in which the Lord chose
him as his prophet. The entire incident points to the fact

that King Uzziah was still alive. The king had been suffering from leprosy for a long time. It is well known that in biblical times leprosy was not regarded merely as one ailment among others, but as the physical symptom of a disturbance in man's relationship to God. Rumour had it that the king had been afflicted because he had presumed to perform sacral functions in the sanctuary at Jerusalem which exceeded his rights as a merely political lieutenant of God. Moreover, Isaiah feels that Uzziah's leprosy was more than a personal affliction, that it symbolized the uncleanliness of the entire people, and Isaiah's own uncleanliness as well. They all have 'unclean lips' (Isaiah 6:5). Like lepers they must all cover 'their upper lip' (Leviticus 13:45) lest by breath or word their uncleanliness go forth and pollute the world. All of them have been disobedient and faithless to the true king, to the king whose glory Isaiah's eyes now behold in his heavenly sanctuary. Here God is called *ha-Melekh* and this is the first time in the Scriptures that he is designated so nakedly, so plainly, as the King of Israel. *He* is the King. The leper whom the people call 'king' is only his faithless lieutenant. And now the true King sends Isaiah with a message to the entire people, at the same time telling him that his message will fail; he will fail, for the message will be misunderstood, misinterpreted and mis-used, and thus confirm the people—save for a small 'remnant'—in their faithlessness, and harden their hearts. At the very outset of the way, Isaiah, the carrier of the spirit, is told that he must fail. He will not suffer disappointment like Plato, for in his case failure is an integral part of the way he must take.[7]

The king of Judah may criticize his backsliding people. The people may criticize their presumptuous king. Only the prophet can effectively and authoritatively criticize them both, his own 'unclean lips' purified by the vision from beyond himself. And as we read, savouring those denunciations as one can only savour the condemnation of other people, Buber quietly but inescapably makes us feel that the words spoken then and there, born into the situation of one time and place, are spoken also here and now, to ourselves in our age and nation:

None but the powerless can speak the true King's will with regard to the state, and remind both the people and the government of their *common* responsibility toward this will. The powerless man can do so because he breaks through the illusions of current history and recognizes potential crises.

That is why his criticism and demands are directed toward society, toward the life men live together. A people which seriously calls God himself its King must become a true people, a community all the members of which are governed by honesty without compulsion, kindness without hypocrisy, and the brotherliness of those who are passionately devoted to their divine Leader. When social inequality, when distinction between the free and the unfree splits the community and creates chasms between its members, there can be no true people, there can be no more 'God's people'. So, the criticism and demands are directed toward every individual on whom other individuals depend, everyone who has a hand in shaping the destinies of others, and that means they are directed toward everyone of us. When Isaiah speaks of justice, he is not thinking of institutions but of you and me, because without you and me, the most glorious institution becomes a lie.[8]

These words, it is true, were first addressed to Jewish students in a Hebrew 'house of study' that Martin Buber helped to found. As published they are addressed to every reader, just as Isaiah's own vision of what lies beyond failure embraces all of us eventually. We may turn to a passage from a piece on 'The Gods of the Nations and God' written three years later, in which Buber focuses in a short paragraph Isaiah's view of the bridging of the gulf between the 'two sides of history'—that of the nations and that of the holy nation:

Amos teaches that all the nations in that they exist in history are concerned with the true God, only that they do not know him. Isaiah supplements the message by saying that they do not know him *as yet*, but that they will know him, for he himself will teach them his ways (Isaiah 2:3). The only advantage we have over them is that we already know him. But this 'already' is what imposes on us the task of preceding them 'in the light of the Lord' (Isaiah 2:5

concluding the prophecy), so that our mountain may be
ready as the goal for the pilgrimage of all. The two sides
have fused into one united world of God. [9]

* * *

The prophet knows that the end of history will be 'one united
world of God'. In this he differs from the apocalyptic vision, also
to be found in the Bible, where there is to be a final separation of
the sheep and the goats to a salvation not in this world but in
another. What is the explanation of this conflict of visions?
Buber's answer is uncompromising. Apocalyptic is not Hebrew in
origin, however much it may become Hebraised (or Hellenized).
It is the alien intrusion of the radical dualism of Light and Darkness, absolute Good and equally absolute Evil, characteristic of
Iranian religion and opposed at the root by the inclusive redemption of the entire Creation which is the final glory of the One God
of Israel, revealed through his prophets, culminating in Isaiah:

> The prophetic belief about the end of time is in all essentials
> autochthonous; the apocalyptic belief is in all essentials
> built up of elements from Iranian dualism. Accordingly,
> the prophetic promises a consummation of creation, the
> apocalyptic its abrogation and supersession by another
> world, completely different in nature; the prophetic
> allows 'the evil' to find the direction that leads toward God,
> and to enter into the good; the apocalyptic sees good and
> evil severed forever at the end of days, the good redeemed,
> the evil unredeemable for all eternity; the prophetic believes
> that the earth shall be hallowed, the apocalyptic despairs of
> an earth which it considers to be hopelessly doomed; the
> prophetic allows God's creative original will to be fulfilled
> completely; the apocalyptic allows the unfaithful creature
> power over the Creator, in that the creatures' actions force
> God to abandon nature. There was a time when it must
> have seemed uncertain whether the current apocalyptic
> teaching might not be victorious over the traditional
> prophetic messianism; if that had happened, it is to be
> assumed that Judaism would not have outlived its central
> faith—explicitly or imperceptibly it would have merged
> with Christianity, which is so strongly influenced by that

dualism. During an epoch in which the prophetic was lacking, the Tannaites, early talmudic masters, helped prophetic messianism to triumph over the apocalyptic conception, and in doing so saved Judaism.[10]

Another danger to the prophetic teaching, one which is also
familiar enough in Middle East religions and by no means unknown in modern thought, is obvious. If everything is destined
to come right in God's good time, or if in the near future some
calamity is certain to befall the more or less faithful, why bother
to exert oneself? Indeed, in the extreme form, human determination to speed up the divine destiny is—as we shall see in the
final chapter—the ultimate danger of dynamic faith. But the
opposite danger, of fatalism, is the 'leave it to the leader' fallacy
carried to its logical limit. The prophetic faith utterly repudiates
fatalism, without, however, falling into the opposite error of
attempting to seize the leadership of the historical process from
God. The passage just quoted, from 'The Two Foci of the Jewish
Soul', continues:

> Still another important difference separates the two forms
> of Jewish belief about the end of days. The apocalyptists
> wished to predict an unalterable immovable future event;
> they were following Iranian conceptions in this point as
> well. For, according to the Iranians, history is divided into
> equal cycles of thousands of years, and the end of the world,
> the final victory of good over evil, can be predetermined
> with mathematical accuracy.
>
> Not so the prophets of Israel: They prophesy 'for the sake
> of those who turn'. (Talmud, Berakhot 34b.) That is, they do
> not warn against something which will happen in any case,
> but against that which will happen if those who are called
> upon to turn do not.[11]

The 'turning' that the people, that we ourselves, are called
upon to make is no mere matter of substituting a theological
'belief that—' for an easygoing polytheism, an agnostic doubtful-
ness or an atheistic disbelief. It is the divine demand that each
man not only acknowledge his own allotted share of responsibility in the redemptive process but exercise it to the limit of his
ability. 'The prophets of Israel', writes Buber, in *Eclipse of God*,

have never announced a God upon whom their hearers' striving for security reckoned. They have always aimed to shatter all security and to proclaim in the opened abyss of the final insecurity the unwished-for God who demands that his human creatures become real, they become human, and confounds all who imagine that they can take refuge in the certainty that the temple of God is in their midst. This is the God of the historical demand as the prophets of Israel beheld Him.[12]

*   *   *

Emphasis on the Law as the social and personal rules that must be obeyed on pain of death or other disagreeable consequences is necessary if an untutored mass of people is not to submerge it altogether in its own disorderly travesty of pure voluntarism. But it also reduces the system, as we saw in Buber's denunciation of what the nations have done to the Ten Commandments, to a caricature of the covenant whose dynamic, on both sides, can only be love. It is the final divorce of outwardness from inwardness in which the Law becomes as much dishonoured in the observance as in the breach. What sort of secular society would it be in which the sole reason why most citizens refrained from murder was fear of the rope or the knife?

The Biblical leader is the man who strives to establish and maintain the Law by pure voluntarism; who will sustain it by force if necessary but will never deceive himself into pretending that such enforcement does not involve another kind of failure. The Hasidic communities, living in exile under alien rule, could not be responsible for all their own affairs, but in the area of living that was within their control they carried voluntarism and personal relationship between leader and led, zaddik and hasidim, further, perhaps, than it has ever been taken in the modern history of the holy nation except, it may be, in some of the pioneer kibbutzim in Israel.

Of the founder of Hasidism, its greatest leader, the Baal Shem, it was said by a 'hidden zaddik'—the highest spiritual authority known to the movement—'if he had lived in the age of the prophets, he would have become a prophet'.[13] The Baal Shem certainly knew from his own experience how leader and led stand or fall together. 'The Erev Rav,' he said, the mixed multitude, prevented Moses from reaching the rung of an angel.[14]

Nevertheless, the zaddik can sometimes break through all the limitations of his group, as seems to be implied in the following Hasidic tale of one of the Baal Shem's grandsons, Barukh of Mezbizh, where the Hasidim play a merely passive role:

> In a certain month of winter, one dark and cloudy night followed upon the other; the moon was hidden and Rabbi Barukh could not say the blessing of the moon. On the last night of those set aside for this, he sent someone out to look at the sky, time after time, but again and again he was told that it was dark as pitch and the snow was falling thick and fast. Finally he said: 'If things were with me as they should be, the moon would surely do me a favour! So I ought to do penance. But because I am no longer strong enough to do it, I must at least penitently confess my sins.' And this penitent confession broke from his lips with such force that all who were there with him were shaken. A great shudder pulsed through their hearts, and they turned to God. Then someone came and reported: 'It isn't snowing any more. You can see a little light!' The rabbi put on his coat and went out. The clouds had scattered. Among the shining stars shone the moon, and he spoke the blessing.[15]

But it is surely no mere coincidence that this is preceded, in the same collection, by another story of the overclouded moon, of which the Baal Shem himself is the central figure, and which emphasizes the role of the led—though the implication may well be that this is the highest achievement of spirtual leadership:

> Once, on the evening after the Day of Atonement, the moon was hidden behind the clouds and the Baal Shem could not go out to say the blessing of the New Moon. This weighed heavily on his spirit, for now, as often before, he felt that destiny too great to be gauged depended on the work of his lips. In vain he concentrated his intrinsic power on the light of the wandering star, to help it throw off the heavy sheath: whenever he sent someone out, he was told that the clouds had grown even more lowering. Finally he gave up hope.

In the meantime, the hasidim who knew nothing of the Baal Shem's grief, had gathered in the front room of the house and begun to dance, for on this evening that was their way of celebrating with festal joy the atonement for the year, brought about by the zaddik's priestly service. When their holy delight mounted higher and higher, they invaded the Baal Shem's chamber, still dancing. Overwhelmed by their own frenzy of happiness they took him by the hands, as he sat there sunk in gloom, and drew him into the round. At this moment, someone called outside. The night had suddenly grown light; in greater radiance than ever before, the moon curved on a flawless sky.[16]

The final emphasis of Hasidism is not on the leader or the led but on the I-Thou relationship that binds them together. It is in this 'between' that God's presence makes itself most unmistakably felt. The tale of 'The Zaddik and his Hasidim'—also in Buber's first volume of *Tales of the Hasidim*—is told by a grandson of another zaddik of the first generation:

In a small town, not far from Tchernobil, several hasidim of my grandfather's were seated together at the conclusion of the sabbath. They were all honest and devout men and at this meal of 'the escort of the queen', they were casting the accounts of their souls. They were so humble and so full of the fear of God, that they thought they had sinned very greatly and agreed that there was no hope for them, and that their only consolation was that they were utterly devoted to the great zaddik Rabbi Nahum, and that he would uplift and redeem them. Then they decided that they must immediately go to their teacher. They started out right after the meal and together they went to Tchernobil. But at the end of that same sabbath, my grandfather was sitting in his house and casting the accounts of his soul. Then in his humility and fear of God, it seemed to him that he had sinned very greatly, and that there was no hope for him except one: that those hasidim, so earnest in the service of God, were so deeply devoted to him, and that they would now comfort him. He went to the door and gazed in the direction his disciples lived, and when he had stood there awhile, he saw them coming.

At this instant—so Rabbi Yitzhak ended his story—two arcs fused to a ring.[17]

Martin Buber often draws attention to a Biblical play upon words. In English, at any rate, it is hard to read that final sentence without being reminded of the arc of the rainbow of the covenant with Noah and the ark of the covenant, with the two golden cherubim between which, it was believed, God was wont to sit enthroned.

*   *   *

Martin Buber begins his account of his favourite Psalm, 73, by emphasizing at some length its message character—'the nature of the prophetic word is introduced into prayer'.[18] This is the essential of prophecy, as he understands it: the goal of prayer is realization of the Presence—but that is not simply the supreme personal gratification, it is that which makes the whole man well up into spontaneous overflow, into radiation whose purpose is to make awareness of the Presence common to all, and specifically 'between man and man'. Usually this cannot be achieved by warnings of disaster impending unless the sinful people 'turn'. Warnings—despite Jonah's trying experience at Nineveh—fail more often than not. It takes actual experience of sheer catastrophe, a destruction of the Temple, a fall of Jerusalem itself, a Babylonian captivity, to reduce most of us to a rudimentary humility in which we are at last disposed seriously to consider what is meant by these moralistic exhortations to 'turn' and even to dabble in it ourselves, until, that is, things seem to be looking up again. This is the main reason why the prophet must fail (with Jonah as the exception to prove the rule) to move all but the receptive few, 'the remnant'. Or rather, he will seem to fail in his own time but not in the true hidden history of the world. 'He must speak his message', Buber declares towards the end of his memorable inaugural lecture on Plato and Isaiah—'The message will be misunderstood, misinterpreted, misused, it will even confirm and harden the people in their faithlessness. But its sting will rankle within them for all time.'[19]

The prophet fails because to succeed he would have to make real for each of his hearers individually the experience of the Presence; and when he speaks of this common goal of the life of prayer—directly, telling others what the Lord has said to them through him—they literally do not know what he is talking about. Or they pay the prophet the ironic compliment of supposing that what is vouchsafed to him will most certainly not be available, and therefore cannot be fundamentally relevant, to them. There is no other way for mankind in the mass than the agonizing experience of history's dramatizations of their ways which are no ways. A profound Hasidic saying uses the parallel—it is much more than metaphor—of labour pains: 'now that redemption is near, no prayer which ascends in behalf of the sorrowful world is of avail, but sorrow is heaped upon sorrow, so that the birth may soon be accomplished'.[20]

The prophet then must be first and foremost a master of prayer; and he must be able, sooner or later, first to the few and in the historical long run to the many, to teach prayer and the goal of prayer—to people to whom (as to very many nowadays) it is either superstitious folly or a sort of unreliable spiritual slot-machine which may sometimes supply on request, in return for a few flattering words, whatever sort of goods one happens to fancy at the time. The whole prophetic vocation—including, since this is true myth, the ultimate happy ending—is implicit in one of the *Tales of Rabbi Nachman*, with which Buber began his renovation of the pure teaching of Hasidism. It is rightly called 'The Master of Prayer'.

The master of prayer in this story converts individuals here and there and brings them to his settlement 'on the shore of the sea' where he betters the Marxist notion of Utopia, treating them all the same by treating each differently but according to 'what each one of his followers needed in order to give him the impulse to holy flight'. But for long he has small success with 'the country of wealth' and its self-deified moguls. However, it so befalls that presently they are besieged by an irresistible conqueror. Strangely enough, this hero is known to the master of prayer. They both once served the same king, who possessed a wonderful figure in the form of a hand. On it was drawn 'each thing as it was at the hour when the world was created, as it has been since then, and as it is today'. We cannot here follow the course of the search in six directions for the missing hand, a narrative of rare beauty and spiritual significance which is the body of the tale. It culminates in the recovery of the king's daughter's lost child, the eternally new-born new beginning:

> The road to the place of the cavern in which the healing food was prepared was now open, for the hand, the tablet of the worlds, was uncovered, and the king again read in it as before. But the king confirmed the word of the wise man: only he who set foot in the place of his own would become cured by it. And so all the comrades exhorted the men from the country of wealth to awaken their wills. Yet none of their words were able to penetrate the deaf hearts.[21]

The child makes them laugh by throwing some of their gold coins in the air and laughing for joy at the fine sight. And the searchers return to bring some semblance of human sanity to their own country. Now the six ways are open, and as this is a Jewish tale we may think of the six-pointed Star of David which is upright from whichever point it is approached, and of its open centre, bounded by the honeycomb cell bases of the six points—the way of the master of prayer. He has now silently disappeared from the tale, but

> each of the king's followers went to his place to renew his strength. And when this had happened and they again had power over the souls of the human race, the king sent them out into all countries, to heal all madness, to enlighten all illusion, and to disentangle all bewilderment and perplexity. The peoples became purified; all turned to the true meaning of life and dedicated themselves to God.[22]

This is probably not a story to suit all modern tastes. Kafka with a happy ending, indeed! One cannot help feeling it would have appealed mightily to Isaiah. But then he was indeed a master of prayer.

*   *   *

We have said that the activity, the wholehearted turning, of the man of prayer—of whom for Buber the writer of Psalm 73 is the great archetype in the Psalms—spontaneously overflows into the message-speaking vocation of the prophet. It is equally inevitable that the particularism of the nation called to be a people of priests—a particularism which exists only to emphasize that the holy nation must itself become such before it can decisively influence the other nations—should issue in the universalism of Isaiah and the later prophets. This is no benevolent afterthought, no altruistic addition to the main business, no incidental consequence of secondary importance; it is the unmistakable sign that the growing point of the individual realization of the Presence everywhere in the creation cannot halt until there is universal realization of the truth that 'the whole world is full of His glory'.

It is often mentioned that Martin Buber joined the emerging Zionist movement while still a student in his early twenties and that he soon took his stand with 'cultural' rather than 'political' Zionism. To understand the basic distinction we need to add Will Herberg's words: 'His Zionism was cultural and spiritual, involving primarily an effort to encourage a renascence of total Jewish existence.'[23] It was certainly not—as we recognized in an earlier chapter—anti-political in the sense that it looked for realization of the Jewish world-mission in exile, without the restoration of the Jewish nation to its own promised land. But, just as the Jewish people had once demanded a monarchy because other nations had one and seemed to thrive on it, so in late nineteenth- and early twentieth-century Europe it seemed to many Jewish philosophers and politicians essential to aim at a secular state (with some traditional flavouring) like the highly 'successful' European nations. For Buber, Zionism could be a nationalism only if it was categorically other than the self-regarding nationalisms of Europe and elsewhere. He writes of

> the struggle between nationalism which denies the spirit of the people and assimilation which denies the body of the people. The overcoming of this dilemma is probably the most difficult task ever imposed on a human community; but we live by and for this task.[24]

The full universal scope of Buber's vision, echoing Isaiah's, is revealed in this piece on 'The Gods of the Nations and God' in *Israel and the World*, written some years before the fateful reappearance of Israel on the map of the world. He is commenting on the work of Nachman Krochmal, the early nineteenth-century originator of the philosophy of Jewish history—who followed Vico, the pioneer of the modern philosphy of history in general, in dividing world history into the history of the nations and that of Israel, to whom alone revelation had been granted:

Krochmal repeatedly tells us that it is our vocation to teach the nations, teach them to worship the absolute in itself, and not the absolutized faculties of the nations. And it is true: we do have to teach this. But how can we teach what we ourselves have not yet learned? A people has only one means to point to God, and that is through life lived in accordance with his will. Up to now, our existence has only sufficed to shake the thrones of the idols, not to erect a throne to God. It is that fact that makes our existence among the nations so mysterious. We pretend to teach the absolute, but what we actually do is say, No, to the other nations, or rather we ourselves are such a negation and nothing more. That is why we have become a nightmare to the nations. That is why every nation is bound to desire to get rid of us at the time it is in the act of setting itself up as the absolute, not only internally—as from time immemorial—but in the order of reality. That is why today we are not permitted to soar over the abyss and point the way to salvation, but are dragged to the bottom of the whirlpool of common wretchedness.[25]

*   *   *

In his first public address to a large gathering in Jerusalem (and again in London soon after the War), Martin Buber spoke of the goal of true history in world-wide Isaianic, terms. He cleansed the organic terms that had been given a sinister meaning by totalitarian exponents of the 'corporate' state and gave them a glory beyond the universal Adam Kadmon of the Kabbalists:

... the world of humanity is meant to become a single body; but it is as yet nothing more than a heap of limbs each of which is of the opinion that it constitutes an entire body. Furthermore, the human world is meant to become a single body through the actions of men themselves. We men are charged to perfect our own portion of the universe— the human world. There is one nation which once upon a time heard this charge so loudly and clearly that the charge penetrated to the very depths of its soul. The nation accepted the charge, not as an inchoate mass of individuals but as a nation. As a nation it accepted the truth which calls for its fulfilment by the human nation, the human race as a whole. And that is its spirit, the spirit of Israel.

The charge is not addressed to isolated individuals but to a nation. For only an entire nation, which comprehends peoples of all kinds, can demonstrate a life of unity and peace, of righteousness and justice to the human race, as a sort of example and beginning. A true humanity, that is, a nation composed of many nations, can only commence with a certain definite and true nation. Only the fulfilment of this truth in the relations between the various sections of this people, between its sects and classes, is capable of serving as a commencement of an international fulfilment of the truth and of the development of a true fellowship of nations, a nation consisting of nations. Only nations each of which is a true nation living in the light of righteousness and justice are capable of entering into upright relations with one another. The people of Israel was charged to lead the way toward this realization.[26]

But, unlike those lofty idealists who do not lower their gaze below the horizon, Buber never forgot that the immediate challenge was always relations with one's neighbours. In political context that meant—the Arabs. As far back as 1921, his contribution to a Zionist congress was an address on behalf of an understanding between Jews and Arabs; and in the political committee he stressed, in opposition to the possibility, which he foresaw, of a federation of Arab states, a Near Eastern Federation in which an autonomous Hebrew community should participate. This might have seemed an easy line to take when there appeared to be small likelihood that a Jewish state would ever again emerge in the Near East. But after his arrival in Palestine he went farther, too far indeed even for such a sympathetic commentator as Arthur Cohen:

> During the strife that accompanied the prelude and consummation of the State of Israel, Buber assumed a position (the natural consequence of his spiritual Zionism) which alienated vast elements of the Israeli community. Arguing with Judah Magnes, Ernst Simon and others, that the only solution to the Jewish problem was a bi-national state in which the Arabs and Jews should jointly participate and share, he aroused great bitterness and resentment.[27]

(Their testimony before the Anglo-American Inquiry Commission, in favour of a bi-national state, has been published.[28]) 'The realities', adds Cohen, 'were not on his side.' The realities of history as success in a struggle for power certainly were not. The realities of ultimate success beyond foreseen failure, the essence of the prophetic faith, await the clearing of the dust-storm of hatred and threats of annihilation with which Israel is now encircled. It must have been in an unguarded moment that a religious Jew thus opposed 'spiritual Zionism' to 'the realities' and came down so hard on the side of the latter. At any rate, the situation that has resulted from trust in political 'realities' certainly constitutes the greatest obstacle to Israel's mission to become a nation indeed, but not as other nations.

Armchair politics is too easy. The terrible holocaust in Europe and the subsequent mass influx of refugees, overrunning all the steady progress that had been made in building up the Jewish population in Palestine in organic small communities, had posed a tragic problem. But, because he believed so much to be at stake, Buber would not compromise:

> Since a Jewish–Arab solidarity had not been instituted, either in the form of facts or even in an announced programme of co-operation, the Arab peoples received the mass immigration as a threat and the Zionist movement as a 'hireling of imperialism'—both wrongly, of course. Our *historical* re-entry into our land took place through a false gateway.[29]

After the stormy establishment of the state, Buber accepted it as 'the form of the new Jewish community that has arisen from the war' but did not relinquish the goal of 'Israel's participation in a Near East Federation'.

> There can be no peace between Jews and Arabs that is only a cessation of war; there can only be a peace of genuine co-operation. Today, under such manifoldly aggravated circumstances, the command of the spirit is still to prepare the way for the co-operation of peoples.[30]

We make no apology for this plunge into a field of intensely controversial politics. Our position is certainly not that Martin Buber was infallible. But remembering how Isaiah's denunciation of great-power alliances in his time was received it may be conceded that, in that sense at least, Buber did not cease to be prophetic when he entered the arena of foreign policy.

* * *

Nor did Buber, in his eightieth year, shrink from direct admonition and warning to the most powerful political leader in the new Israel. The second edition of *Israel and the World* concludes with his answer to an address to the 1957 Jerusalem Ideological Conference by David Ben-Gurion. Buber reminded the Conference that in Israel alone the prophets dared to stand before the king

> and censure him for betraying his mission and prophesy that calamity will befall him if he does not mind his ways and does not fulfil the obligations assumed in the act of being anointed. This mission they performed at the risk of their lives. This is the transcendental realism which distinguishes the faith of Israel: there is no room here for empty symbols.
>
> What exactly was it that the prophets censured when they faced the rulers? It was the means they used to arrive at their ultimate goal, concerning which the prophets did not differ—the glory of Israel. These means contradicted the ends, and one of the unexpressed principles of prophecy is that ends do not justify the means. And if the nature of the means is in contradiction to the nature of the end, they desecrate it, poison it and make of it a thing of horror.[31]

He reminded Ben-Gurion that Isaiah not only called upon the Gentiles to stream to Mount Zion—he summoned the House of Jacob to walk before them in the light of the Lord. Then followed the direct denunciation:

> Behind everything that Ben-Gurion has said on that point, there lies, it seems to me, the will to make the political factor supreme. He is one of the proponents of that kind of secularization which cultivates its 'thoughts' and 'visions' so diligently that it keeps men from hearing the voice of the living God. This secularization takes the form of an exaggerated 'politization'. This 'politization' of life here

strikes at the very spirit itself. The spirit with all its thoughts and visions descends and becomes a function of politics. This phenomenon, which is supreme in the whole world at present, has very old roots. Even some kings in Israel are said to have gone so far as to employ false prophets whose prophesying was merely a function of state policy.[32]

Ben-Gurion had stated that Zionism no longer had a real or positive content. Buber answered that quasi-Zionism which strove to have a country only had attained its purpose:

> But the true Zionism, the love of Zion, the desire to establish something like 'the city of a great king' (Psalm 48:3), of 'the king' (Isaiah 6:5), is a living and enduring thing. Come, let us awaken this Zionism in the hearts that have never felt it, in the Diaspora as well as here . . .[33]

Finally he dealt with what he regarded as Ben-Gurion's 'politization' of the Messianic message itself:

> And now Ben-Gurion tells us that Zionist thought is dead but that the Messianic idea is alive and will live until the coming of the Messiah. And I answer him with the question: 'In how many hearts of this generation in our country does the Messianic idea live in a form other than the narrow nationalistic form which is restricted to the Ingathering of the Exiles?' A Messianic idea without the yearning for the redemption of mankind and without the desire to take part in its realization, is no longer identical with the Messianic visions of the prophets of Israel, nor can the prophetic mission be identified with a Messianic ideal emptied of belief in the coming of the kingdom of God.[34]

We do not equate Martin Buber with Isaiah. But we can hardly read these words of burning sincerity without realizing that here was a man who accepted not only in mind and imagination but in his very bones and blood the spirit of the prophetic faith as he knew it and to the utmost limit of his own capacity.

THE WAY: THE SERVANT

THERE is an early Jewish tradition that Isaiah was sawn asunder. However that may be there is now general agreement that the Book of Isaiah is in two nearly equal parts, separated by considerably more than a century. Isaiah's name does not occur after the end of the first part (chapter 38). In the second, there are no more allusions to 'the remnant' whose turning will mitigate the general failure to heed the words of the prophet. Hopes of ultimate success from the long experiment in monarchy are virtually abandoned; the Messiah is no longer to be a king but 'the servant'. The servant is mentioned only in Deutero–Isaiah.

Buber writes at length on this culmination of the prophetic teaching, in *The Prophetic Faith*. We quote here a more summary statement from *Two Types of Faith*:

As the kings fail to fulfil their task, the prophets reply with the prediction about the coming one who will fulfil the anointing. With the break-up of the Judean Kingdom the old Messianic hope becomes problematic. It is not destroyed by it, indeed it springs up afresh with the first movement for return, but in the meantime a new, quite unheard-of form has appeared on the scene, the proclaimer of which treated the former as historically settled. The Messianic commission in its actual form was divided by him into two during the period of suffering in the Exile: the task of beginning, the leading back of Israel to its land is now transferred to a foreign prince, Cyrus, as YHVH's anointed (Isaiah 45:1), but the actual commission—and with it the fulfillment of the 'new' prophecy against the 'first' one—the establishmnet of the righteous community of Israel as the centre of the freed nations of the world devolves upon the new man from Israel, upon the 'servant of YHVH'. The commission to him embraces two functions, two phases, which are divided among different persons, who however represent only two manifestations of the same figure; this becomes ever more clear to us as we proceed from one to the other of the four songs (42:1–9, 49:1–9a, 50:4–9, 52:13–53:12), and so apparently the prophet himself gained increasing clarity through his experiences and disappointments. The first function, which is preparatory, is suffering: the 'servant' of the period of suffering takes upon himself in his own present condition of prophetic concealment the burden of the sins of the 'many' from the nations of the world, he who is guiltless exculpates them and thereby makes possible the speedy breaking-through of salvation (if the reading in the Masoretic text 'in his deaths' may be accepted, as I think, then earlier suffering prophets may be regarded as manifestations of the servant). The second function, the Messianic fulfillment, is reserved for another, public appearance of the 'servant'; then for the first time will the nations of the world with Israel recognize how and through whom the preparation took place. (Essential to the understanding is that the one appointed for public recognition remains in the 'quiver' until he is drawn out, i.e. this his special Messianic vocation can be surmised indeed beforehand, but not actually known.)[1]

The suggestion of a continuous line, a spiritual succession of 'servants' which is to culminate in the Messiah is, for obvious historical reasons, generally resisted in Jewish traditional teaching. 'According to rabbinic teaching', records the *Standard Jewish Encyclopaedia,*

> the spirit of prophecy ceased with the last of the Minor Prophets (Zechariah, etc.), the spiritual role of the prophet thereafter being assumed by the 'Men of the Great Synagogue' and the sages who succeeded them. These had the faculty of interpreting the Bible prophecies; indeed 'a Sage is higher than a Prophet' (*Baba Batra* 12a). In the messianic age, however, the faculty of prophecy would be renewed.[2]

Gordis contrasts the Christian and Jewish reactions to Deutero–Isaiah, the latter merging the figure of the 'servant' in the corporate destiny of Israel:

> ... the fifty-third chapter of Isaiah, which depicts the suffering servant of the Lord, has been regarded in tradi-

tional Christian circles as a prophecy of the career of Jesus. It has therefore played an incalculable role in Christian thought. On the other hand, Jewish commentators, like many Christian exegetes, have interpreted it as a portrayal of the tragic-heroic function of the people of Israel as God's witnesses in a pagan world. Yet the moving figure of the suffering servant, which has had such an impact on the Christian conception of the Saviour, never became equally basic to the traditional Jewish world view. Thus, practically none of the beautiful 'Servant Songs' were chosen for the *Haftarot*, the prophetic readings in the synagogue liturgy.[3]

There is, nevertheless, another tradition, whose root is traced to the Talmud. Buber, in a note, summarizes it thus:

> Thirty-six Hidden Zaddikim: the Talmud (Sukkah 45b) speaks of the thirty-six pious men who welcome the presence of God every day; in later legends they are described as humble, unrecognized saints. Disguised as peasants, artisans, or porters, they go around doing good deeds. They constitute the true 'foundation of the world'.[4]

For a fuller and more picturesque version of this myth, we may refer to the remarkable novel by André Schwarz-Bart, *The Last of the Just*, where it is to be noted that the Talmudic reference is explicitly referred to the times of Isaiah:

> ... the ancient Jewish tradition of the *Lamed-waf*, a tradition that certain Talmudists trace back to the source of the centuries, to the mysterious times of the prophet Isaiah. Rivers of blood have flowed, columns of smoke have obscured the sky; but surviving all these dooms, the tradition has remained inviolate down to our times. According to this tradition the world reposes upon thirty-six Just Men, the *Lamed-waf*, indistinguishable from simple mortals; often, they do not recognize themselves. But if even one of them were lacking, the sufferings of mankind would poison even the souls of the new-born, and humanity would suffocate with a single cry. For the *Lamed-waf* are the hearts of the world multiplied, into which all our griefs are poured, as into one receptacle. They occur in thousands of popular stories. Their presence is attested everywhere. A very old

text of the Hagadah tells us that the most pitiable are the *Lamed-waf* who remain unknown to themselves. For these, the spectacle of the world is an unspeakable hell. In the seventh century, Andalusian Jews venerated a rock shaped like a teardrop, which they believed to be the soul of an 'unknown' *Lamed-waf*. Other *Lamed-waf*, like Hecuba shrieking at the death of her sons, are said to have been transformed into dogs. 'When an Unknown Just rises to Heaven,' a Hasidic story goes. 'he is so frozen that God must warm him for a thousand years between His fingers, before his soul can open itself to Paradise. And it is known that some remain for ever inconsolable at human woe; so that even God Himself cannot warm them. So from time to time the Creator, Blessed be his Name, sets the clock of the Last Judgment forward by one minute.'[5]

Here, of course, is myth running riot. But the very guarded Talmudic source cannot be disputed and the luxuriance of the later popular tradition shows what hold this legend of a secret 'succession' took upon the Jewish spirit.

In an important passage of *The Prophetic Faith*, which must also be quoted here at some length, Buber deals with the problem of the personal, group or national identity of 'the servant', or rather of the intimate relation between these: 'The suffering *nabi*' (prophet) he writes, 'is the antecedent type of the acting Messiah.

Perhaps we may see here the explanation of the enigmatical epithet of the servant, *meshullam* (Isaiah 42:19). *Meshullam*, that is to say 'the perfected one', he is called after the maturity of his vocation, inasmuch as he is sent by God as His 'messenger' to the world of nations. The fact that he is called in this place 'blind' and 'deaf' is apparently to be explained by the fact that at the moment God speaks he, the *nabi*, has not yet proved able to grasp his own destiny and the way to its accomplishment in spite of his many experiences and of the fact that his ears are open to receive God's word. His readiness to serve in his appointment is in advance of his 'knowledge' (53:11; a colon must be put after this word: the servant recognizes and knows the intention of God concerning him that is expressed in the following verses). Deutero–Isaiah sees himself as the figure the servant assumes in the hour of knowledge, the hour when the great connection of things is made known.

Admittedly the aforementioned verse about *meshullam* belongs to the verses which speak of the servant of Israel and of the personal servant in the same expressions, and the dividing line between them appears somewhat blurred. So there are passages before this (42:16, 18) speaking of the people as blind and deaf, as this passage speaks of the blind and deaf servant. But just as we must nevertheless distinguish between them, so on the other hand we cannot overcome the difficulty by the supposition of later additions or alterations. The prophet wishes us never to forget the special tie between the personal servant and the servant Israel. They are closely fastened one to the other. The personal servant is that Israel in whom YHVH glorifies himself as in His faithful one (49:3), but just because he is that, YHVH can glorify himself in Israel generally as in that which is redeemed by Him (44:23). YHVH's love for faithless Israel, a hurt and suffering love, renews itself from the prophet's love of God, a love hurt and suffering for God's sake. There is a nucleus of Israel, preserved through the generations, that does not betray the election, that belongs to God and remains His. Through this nucleus the living connection between God and the people is upheld, in spite of the very great guilt: not alone by interposing on behalf of Israel, but far more by being the true Israel. God's purpose for Israel has put on skin and flesh in these powerless combatants. They are the small beginning of the kingdom of God before Israel becomes a beginning of it; they are the beginning before the beginning. The anointing of the kings was unfulfilled, and Deutero–Isaiah no longer awaits a king in whom this anointing should be fulfilled: the anointing of the *nebiim* has been fulfilled, and therefore it is from their midst that the figure of the perfected one will arise. All that the *nabi* in this his ultimate form shall establish in the world of the nations, Israel shall establish by him. For through him, through his word and life, Israel turns to God, and becomes God's people. No more will these two, Israel and the prophet, be opposed one to the other, and there will not even be any more distinction between them. Now not only, as up to this time, the truth of Israel, but the reality of Israel in its purity, will be embodied in the *nabi*, the reality of *Jeshurun* (44:2), the upright people, in the reality of *Meshullam*, the perfected one. At the same hour when this man is allowed to go up, after persevering again and again in the hiddenness and migrating through afflictions and deaths unto true life; when he is allowed to go up and be a light for the nations, at that hour the servant Israel and the personal servant will have become one. [6]

*   *   *

We have spoken earlier of the opposite dangers: of a quietism which, in the face of all human sin and intolerable suffering and misery, 'piously' resolves to leave it all to God to solve; and of the desperate courage, born of determination that all this wretchedness is no longer to be borne, which will even dare to coerce God, attempt to 'force the end'. Where, between these extremes, is the perfected balance of utmost effort and also acceptance of the essential limitation of man, who may never 'take over the leadership' from God? We can understand that it is the way that prepares for the emergence of the Messiah. Beyond that the way is hidden in the uttermost depths of the soul of Israel and in the incomprehensible will of God. This is the secret dialogue which remains concealed until it ends in the ending of what we have chosen to call history.

The story of Jesus of Nazareth appears to Buber to be that of a giant of the spirit who was indeed involved in that secret dialogue and who judged—or rather, in the last analysis mis-judged—that that final fateful hour had come upon the world. The impulse that produced that misjudgment was a love of man, of a purity the like of which has hardly been disclosed in human history. That was why it *had* to be Now. Martin Buber could never allow the divisions of creeds to stand between him and the love of this man; nor would he be tempted to be blinded by that love into an acceptance of the Pauline deification which marks the real frontier between Christianity and Judaism. 'From my youth onwards', he writes in the Foreword to *Two Types of Faith*, the beautiful book in which he accepts his human Jesus and rejects the God-man of the Churches,

I have found in Jesus my great brother ... My own
fraternally open relationship to him has grown ever stronger
and clearer, and today I see him more strongly and clearly
than ever before.[8]

'See'—in such a context—is not a word that Martin Buber
would use lightly. We may remember the solemnity with which
he uses the word in recalling those Germans who died rather than
tolerate the holocaust of Jews in our time: 'I see these men very
near before me in that especial intimacy which binds us at times
to the dead and to them alone.'[8]

Buber does not only love Jesus. He tries to understand him in
relation to the great tradition of Jewish prophecy. He does not
avoid, as some Jewish authorities understandably do, the striking
affinities between Deutero–Isaiah and Jesus. Nor does he, as
Christianity does, identify Jesus with the Messiah who was to be
drawn from 'the quiver' at the time known only to God. What he
does clearly see is the profound influence upon Jesus himself of
the Deutero–Isaianic prophecies. He does not presume to
question that Jesus was entitled to regard himself as in the
spiritual succession of concealed suffering servants. The problem
is rather whether, under the influence of Biblical apocalyptic
(which, we have noted, Buber rejects as unHebraic in essence)
Jesus did not finally endeavour through his sacrifice to impose his
own will on that of God, draw himself from the quiver—thereby
causing a sort of spiritual nuclear explosion that has indeed been
a light to the nations for two thousand years, but whose effects on
the concentrated continuity of the 'servant' whose time has not
yet come we cannot know or conjecture.

> If we view the connexion rightly Jesus understood himself,
> under the influence of the conception of Deutero–Isaiah, to
> be a bearer of the Messianic hiddenness. From this follows
> straightway the meaning of the 'Messianic secret'. The
> arrow in the quiver is not its own master; the moment at
> which it shall be drawn out is not for it to determine. The
> secret is imposed. It is put by Jesus into the heart of the
> disciples—whose confession indeed confirms him in it—like
> Isaiah once 'sealed up' the message of salvation in the heart
> of his own. Only when in sight of the end does the attitude of
> Jesus appear to change.[9]

It changes, that is, to an identification-experience with the Messiah who is to come. As Buber would locate the genuine historical nucleus of Mark 14:62, Jesus at his trial has just been asked 'Who art thou?'—as he earlier had asked his disciples—

> but he, looking into realms beyond, replies in effect: 'Thou shalt see the one whom I shall become.' *He* sees him now: I am he. He does not say it, but there are those who hear him who mean to hear it, because they see him, the one who sees. That he imagines himself in his own person as the one who will be removed and afterwards sent again to an office of fulfillment, in the figure of the vision of Daniel, is suggested strongly enough. The one who is now removed from the state of concealment and thereupon entering not a further concealment, but a Messianic revelation, must come from above, since now he is equipped with the other real- izing power which was not granted him in the former state: he who experienced the lack of this power cannot think of it any more as confined within earthly conditions. If we may presuppose such a change of view, then the biographical fact is given, around which after the death of Jesus and the visions of the disciples the crystallizing of the mythical element lying ready in the hearts of those influenced by Hellenism took place, until the new binitarian God-image was present. Not merely new symbols but actually new images of God grow up from human biography and precisely from its most unpremeditated moments.[10]

It may be seriously asked whether any deeper or more under- standing insight into the experience of Jesus in his last hours has been expressed by any other writer in modern times. Buber's gaze is clear, fearless and loving. But it does not waver. God is One.

*   *   *

In an earlier chapter, we saw a certain geographical parallel between the eighteenth-century Poland in which Hasidism arose only shortly before Poland disappeared from the map and Biblical Palestine, similarly caught between the fell incensed points of mighty opposites. If the phenomena of 'hidden zaddiks' and Messianic temptation were also familiar to and in Hasidism, that may well be because the parallel extends a good deal farther, into the actual and intolerable conditions of the time and place. Less than a century before the Baal Shem was born, the Jewish people had endured terrible suffering and in many places extermination, on a scale unprecedented until recent times, at the hands of the fanatical and barbaric Cossacks. Again we must resort to brief factual summary. In 1648, the Cossack leader Chmielnitzki headed the rising of the Cossacks and Ukrainian masses

> directed against the Polish landowners, the Catholic clergy and the Jews. The rebellion initially made headway and resulted in the annihilation of hundreds of Jewish communities and the brutal murder of hundreds of thousands of Jews, only those accepting baptism being spared. The exact number cannot be ascertained but one contemporary source affirms that 744 communities were wiped out. The horror of these events sent a shock throughout Jewry and the consequent Messianic impulse served to gather support for Shabbetai Tzevi. The Ukrainians regard Chmielnitzki as a national hero.[11]

Less than twenty years afterwards Shabbetai Tzevi, or Sabbatai Zevi—as it is usually rendered—proclaimed his Messianic mission and though this soon led to his renunciation of Judaism and adoption of Islam he had gained wide adherence and in fact his sect, the Donmeh, still lingers on. The reason why his defection to Islam did not put an end to it seems to be that this was represented as the way to 'liberate the sparks' from the as yet unredeemed nations. Sabbatai's harrowing of hell made use of the *Zohar*'s belief that the Messiah would be good within and evil without. He was followed in the next century by Jacob Frank, whose movement made a point of abandoning the Law for a moral anarchism that seems at times to have been orgiastic. 'The gospel of antinomianism preached by Jacob Frank,' says Scholem, whose *Major Trends in Jewish Mysticism* is valuable on both these messianic pretenders, was 'in more than two thousand dogmatic sayings. The ideas he adduced in support of his preachings constitute not so much a theory as a veritable *religious myth of nihilism*.'[12] Frank and his followers were baptized as Christians in the year before the Baal Shem died, 1759. However tragically absurd we may take these phenomena to be, the conditions under which they flourished demanded some relief. There was, understandably, a counter-reaction among the rabbis which, at its worst, resulted in unconsoling insistence on every jot and tittle of the Law. The greater the Jewish heart, however, the harder it must have been to preach only patience and obedience to panic-stricken and poverty-stricken masses in a state of religious upheaval. The little Hasidic communities, with their emphasis on joyous living together, were tiny islands in a sea of misery. It was not for a man like the Baal Shem Tov to content himself with the pious and philosophical reflection that this was all that could be expected in the circumstances. He too knew the Messianic temptation.

Buber's early allusion to this is wrapped in mystery. But the role of 'Rabbi Zvi the scribe, his disciple' who acts in effect as the tempter to the Baal Shem to persist in his attempt to reach Jerusalem (in the story of that name in *The Legend of the Baal Shem*)[13] against the decree of the Lord but driven by 'the lamentation of the voices' that 'rode like a storm in the air' seems to be the mythic interpretation of the Baal Shem's encounter with the Messianic temptation that overcame Sabbatai Zevi. At any rate, the position is directly treated in the first volume of *Tales of the Hasidim*. There again 'Rabbi Zevi' appears, in a strange story of his entry with the Baal Shem into a wood. The only observer is discovered and sent away—'No one has ever found out what happened in the wood after that.' But this is followed almost at once—only the already quoted saying of the Baal Shem about how the 'mixed multitude' prevented even Moses from reaching the rung of an angel intervening—by a story explicitly called 'The Temptation':

It is told:
Sabbatai Zevi, the 'false Messiah' long dead, came to the Baal Shem and begged him to redeem him. Now it is well known that the work of redemption is accomplished by binding the stuff of life, by binding mind to mind, and soul to soul. In this way, then, the Baal Shem began to bind himself to that other, but slowly and cautiously, for he feared he might try to harm him. Once, when the Baal Shem lay asleep, Sabbatai Zevi came and tried to tempt him

to become as he himself was. Then the Baal Shem hurled him away with such vigour that he fell to the very bottom of the nether world. When the Baal Shem spoke of him, he always said: 'A holy spark was within him, but Satan caught him in the snare of pride.[14]

Some light is thrown on what is meant by saying that the 'false Messiah' who drew himself out of the quiver (or rather who was not really in it but presumed he was) had a 'holy spark' within him by a story of one of the later masters of Hasidism. It is no accident that this tale is told of one whose real name certainly was Yehudah Zevi, of Stretyn. This expresses the belief that the line of servants still runs through the concealment, so that one may legitimately speak of the Messiah, or perhaps of the 'growing' Messiah, as living among us:

> A hasid told this story:
> 'Once Rabbi Yehudah Zevi said to us at table: "Today Messiah the son of Joseph will be born in Hungary, and he will become one of the hidden zaddikim. And if God lets me live long enough, I shall go there and see him."
> 'Eighteen years later the rabbi travelled to the city of Pest and took me with him along with other hasidim. We stayed in Pest for several weeks and not one of us disciples knew why we had come.
> 'One day a youth appeared at the inn. He wore a short coat and his face was as beautiful as an angel's. Without asking permission he went straight into the rabbi's room and closed the door behind him. I remembered those words I had heard long ago, kept near the door, and waited to greet him as he came out and ask his blessing. But when hours later he did come out, the rabbi accompanied him to the gate, and when I ran out into the little street, he had vanished. Even now after so many years, my heart still beats with the living impulse I received from him as he went by.'[15]

*   *   *

Messianic temptation does not only take the form of self-identification with the Messiah and self-proclamation. Not long

after the death of the Baal Shem, the apotheosis of self-chosen
human leadership, the first ominous modern man of destiny, cast
his shadow over all Europe: Napoleon. The continent became
convulsed in war. What form did the crying of the human heart
for peace take in the inmost circle of Hasidism? The strange and
haunting answer is summarized in Buber's Foreword to the
Jewish Publication Society edition of the chronicle-novel *For
The Sake of Heaven*:

> It is a fact that several Zaddikim actually attempted by
> means of theurgic or magic activities (the so-called Practical
> Kabbalah) to make of Napoleon that 'Gog of the Land of
> Magog', mentioned by Ezekiel, whose wars, as is pro-
> claimed by several eschatological texts, were to precede the
> coming of the Messiah. Other Zaddikim opposed these
> attempts with the monition that no outer gestures or events
> but only the inner return of the entire human being to God
> could prepare the approach of redemption. And what is so
> extraordinary and remarkable is the fact that all these men,
> both magicians and monitors, actually died within the
> space of a single year. Thus there can be little doubt that the
> spiritual sphere in which they were involved, although from
> different sides, consumed their mortal being. Hence it is not
> a legendary symbol but a simple fact of experience that in
> this conflict both sides were annihilated.[16]

The protagonists were, on the theurgic side, Yaakov Yitzhak,
the 'Seer of Lublin' (d. 1815) and, very strangely, another
Yaakov Yitzhak, of Pshysha, the 'Holy Yehudi', on the side of
the 'turning'. Buber was 'for' Pshysha and 'against' Lublin, but
he had to try 'to penetrate the kernel from both sides'.

He early came to know the traditions and anecdotes handed
down by both schools and—the historical context is once again
deeply significant—during the last year of World War I familiar-
ized himself with the physical scenes in which the events had
taken place a hundred years before. But two attempts to write the
history of them in a way that would bring the spiritual issue to
urgent and contemporary life failed. It was only later, in
Jerusalem, under the terrible impact of the beginning of World
War II, that the book virtually wrote itself, in Hebrew.

Its appearance, and subsequently that of the English translation, led to various misunderstandings of his purpose, one of which particularly concerns us here. It is the last that Buber deals with in his Foreword:

> Another reproach that was addressed to me was that, whether consciously or not, I had changed the figure of the Holy Yehudi under the sway of a 'Christianizing tendency'. I may reply that I have described no single trait of this man which does not exist in the tradition, which also includes those sayings of his that remind one of some in the Gospels. Whatever in this book the Yehudi may have in common with Jesus of Nazareth derives, not from a tendency, but from a reality. It is the reality of the suffering 'servants of the Lord'. In my opinion the life of Jesus cannot be understood if one does not recognize the fact that he—as has been pointed out by Christian theologians too, especially by Albert Schweitzer—stood in the shadow of the concept of the 'servant of the Lord' as we find it in the Deutero–Isaiah. But he emerged from the hiddenness of the 'quiver' (Isaiah 49:2), while the Holy Yehudi remained within it. It is necessary to visualize the hand which first sharpens the arrow and then slips it into the darkness of the quiver, and the arrow which huddles in the darkness.[17]

Only now are we in a position to understand the end of the Foreword that Buber wrote to his book on Jesus, *Two Types of Faith*, ten years after he wrote *For the Sake of Heaven* (of which the original title is *Gog and Magog*). Living in Jerusalem, a virtually helpless spectator of the destruction of European Jewry and much of Europe in the Second World War, Buber had indeed come to feel on his pulses and in his heart the desperate longing to bring good out of ultimate evil by 'hastening the end'—but still he somehow held to the 'side' of Pshysha. Now fighting broke into Jerusalem itself, it seemed that only a miracle could prevent the Jewish resettlers and survivors being swept into the sea and the sole historic chance of Israel arising into full nationhood on her own holy soil from being lost. Now Buber could feel something of the Messianic temptation that he believed had finally overcome Jesus of Nazareth. His half-century study of the New Testament took fire. This is how we may understand the words with which he closes the Foreword, dated Jerusalem—Talbiyeh,

January 1950. (Talbiyeh is a predominantly Arab quarter of Jerusalem.)

> I wrote this book in Jerusalem during the days of its so-called siege, or rather in the chaos of destruction which broke out within it. I began it without a plan, purely under the feeling of a commission, and in this way chapter after chapter has come into being. The work involved has helped me to endure in faith this war, for me the most grievous of the three.[18]

But, as the book reveals, he somehow remained on the side of Pshysha. And the military miracle happened, the Jews withstood their assailants, the State of Israel was declared. With that epoch-making event, it seemed to Martin Buber, came a decisive step forward on the road of true history, however much its face was marred and blackened by atrocity and false motive. The brief introduction to the three addresses on Judaism, *At the Turning*, which he gave in New York at the end of 1951, concludes:

> The reader should bear in mind, that a Jew speaks here to Jews, in the centre of the Diaspora, in the hour when the deciding crisis of Judaism begins to become manifest.

In the second lecture, 'The Silent Question' he said:

> I have recently received communications from many parts of the world from which it can be sensed that clarification and leadership are expected of Judaism. It can be sensed, too, that many of these correspondents are speaking for the many more who remain silent. That the world expects something from Judaism is in itself a new phenomenon. For centuries, the deeper spiritual content of Judaism was either unknown or given scant attention, for the reason perhaps that, during the period of the ghetto, the underlying reality of Jewish life was hardly glimpsed by the outside world, while during the emancipation period, Jews only— not Judaism—appeared upon the open scene.
>
> A change seems to be taking place. Why? Is it because of the massacre of millions of Jews? That does not explain it. Or is it because of the establishment of a Jewish State? That does not explain it either. And yet both of these events are basically part of the reason why the real content of Judaism

is beginning to become more perceptible. These astounding phenomena of dying and living have at last brought before the world the fact of the existence of Jewry as a fact of particular significance, and from this point Judaism itself begins to be seen. Now the world has gradually begun to perceive that within Judaism there is something which has its special contribution to make, in a special way, to the spiritual needs of the present time. It is only possible to realize this if Judaism is regarded in its entirety, in its whole way, from the Decalogue to Hasidism, in the course of which its peculiar tendencies have evolved in an increasingly comprehensive manner.[19]

These are the words of a man who profoundly believes that prophecy did not cease with Zechariah, that the 'servants' are among us—however we are to picture the reality within that persistent myth—and have grown in strength through two thousand years of concealment.

* * *

Our ending takes us back to our beginning, to the Book of Genesis. We quoted, in another chapter, the Hasidic way of putting the truth of the multiplicity and malleability of human nature and potentiality, that each man had within him the elements of various Biblical characters good and bad. And it is by looking for the traits suggested by the Biblical portraits of Adam, Noah, Abraham, Moses, the Psalmist and Isaiah that we have found tides running deep and strong through the teaching of Martin Buber, merging, it is hoped, into a still recognizable unique human personality. But if we suppose that he was at any time consciously playing the part of one or other of these Biblical figures, we mistake him altogether.

Of the twenty-two addresses in the original edition of *Israel and the World*, the same number as that of the letters of the Hebrew alphabet in which all its Torah was written, Buber says in the Preface that only one was not written to meet the needs of a particular moment. The one that least of all bears the mark of time is called 'Imitatio Dei'. It was written in 1926, not long after *I and Thou*, when he had just begun to work with the paralysed Franz Rosenzweig on the translation of the Hebrew Bible.

In effect it asks and answers the basic question: how should we endeavour to shape our lives? It considers three answers, which are essentially: those of Greek paganism, Christianity and Judaism. These models are: God represented in perfected human form, the Zeus of Phidias; the God-man, Christ; and God Himself, who is 'invisible, incomprehensible, unformed, not-to-be-formed'. The last, Buber notes, was not unknown to the early Church; as distinct from the imitation of Christ which reached its zenith in Francis of Assisi, there was the injunction of Ignatius of Antioch in his Epistle to the Philadelphians: 'Be ye followers of Jesus Christ, as he was a follower of his Father.' That is to say, the true imitation of Jesus would not be imitation of him but imitation of God Himself.

But the question is still unanswered. How to imitate the 'not-to-be-formed' Deity, the One God? The answer may be found only in the original gift of God to Man in his creation:

> 'For in the image of God made He Man.' It is on this that the imitation of God is founded.[20]

That he may not be misunderstood, Buber has prefaced this with a vital distinction:

> . . . we may well add that the perfection of a soul is called its being like God, which yet does not mean any equality, but means that this soul has translated into reality that likeness to God which was granted it. We perfect our souls 'toward' God; this means that each of us who does this makes perfect *his* likeness to God, his *yehida*, his soul, his 'only one', his uniqueness *as* God's image.[21]

Adam was both right and wrong. He succumbed to a dream of becoming godlike; but had not understood what Buber called an unexpressed doctrine of the prophets, that the means determine the end:

> The Fall of the first human being consisted in his wanting to reach the likeness intended for him in his creation by other means than by perfecting 'the image'.[22]

And once this is understood there is no reason why we may not simply say, as Buber quotes from a hasidic book, that 'The fundamental reason for the creation of man is that he is to make himself as much like his Creator as he can'.[23] And long before the

Hasidim, a Talmudic master, Abba Shaul, had commented on the text 'Ye shall be holy; for I the Lord your God am holy'—'It behooves the royal retinue to imitate the King.'

Still the question is without its final answer. How is a man to develop in the image in which he had been formed, to find his individual way? Buber replies with words from Jewish classical teaching on a text from Deuteronomy which Schecter called 'Israel's book of *imitatio dei*'. The text is 'To love the Lord your God, to walk in all His ways.' And here we will have done with all selection, rearrangement and exposition, and let Martin Buber speak to the end. He quotes the text from Deuteronomy and adds, from Sifre on the verse (11:22):

'What are the ways of God? Those which He himself proclaimed to Moses: "God, merciful, gracious, long-suffering, abundant in lovingkindness and faithfulness."' Another saying is still more explicit: 'After the Lord your God shall ye walk' (Deuteronomy 13:5); how should man be able to walk in the footsteps of the Divine Presence? Is it not written (Deuteronomy 4:24): 'The Lord thy God is a devouring fire?' But the meaning is: Follow after the *middot*, the 'attributes', still better, the modes in which God works as far as these are made known to man. As he clothed the nakedness of the first human beings, as he visited the sick Abraham in the grove at Mamre (where according to tradition Abraham suffered the pangs of circumcision), as he comforted Isaac with his blessing after Abraham's death, until the last act of God in the Pentateuch, when he himself buried Moses—all these are enacted *middot*, visible patterns for man, and the *mitzvot*, the commandments, are *middot* made human. 'My handicraft,' as the Midrash has God say to Abraham, 'is to do good—you have taken up my handicraft.'

The secret of God which stood over Job's tent (Job 29:4), before it grew fearfully into his suffering and questioning, can only be fathomed by suffering, not by questioning, and man is equally forbidden to question and to imitate these secret ways of God. But God's handicraft, his revealed way of working, has been opened before us and set up for us as a pattern.

Thus it was not vouchsafed to Moses to see God's 'face', but he learned his 'ways', which God himself proclaimed, when he passed by before him; and this proclamation God calls the proclamation of his 'Name'.

But where are the revealed ways of God's working revealed?

Just at the beginning of the wandering through the desert; just at the height of Job's trial; just in the midst of the terror of the other, the incomprehensible, ununderstandable works; just from out of the secret. God does not show mercy and grace alone to us; it is terrible when his hand falls on us, and what then happens to us does not somehow find a place *beside* mercy and grace, it does not belong to the same category as these; the ultimate does not belong here to the attribute of righteousness—it is beyond all attributes. It is indeed the secret, and it is not for us to enquire into it. But just in this quality of God's is his 'handiwork' manifested to us. Only when the secret no longer stands over our tent, but breaks it, do we learn to know God's intercourse with us. And we learn to imitate God.[24]

BOOK LIST

No complete edition of the collected works of Martin Buber has yet appeared in English.

In German there is now a definitive edition in three volumes (Munich: Kosel and Heidelberg: Schneider).

Martin Buber, *Werke*:
Erster Band: Schriften zur Philosophie, 1962 (1128 pp.)
Zweiter Band: Schriften zur Bibel, 1964 (1235 pp.)
Dritter Band: Schriften zum Chassidismus, 1963 (1270 pp.)

Associated with this is another large volume of collected works: *Der Jude und sein Judentum*. Gesammelte Aufsätze und Reden. Mit einer Einleitung von Robert Weltsch. Cologne: Joseph Melzer.

English translations and editions of works by Martin Buber are listed in the following Notes and References. For complete listing and Hebrew and German original publication, see:

A Bibliography of Martin Buber's Works: 1895–1957. Compiled by Moshe Catanne. Jerusalem: The Bialik Institute, 1958.

NOTE: Published on the occasion of M.B.'s eightieth birthday. But the date is given incorrectly on the English title-page (as February 4) and correctly in Hebrew as February 8.

ABBREVIATIONS USED IN NOTES AND REFERENCES
(* indicates editions used)

Abbreviations all in capitals are book titles. Abbreviations in which the initial capital is followed by letters in lower case are items in a book or periodical whose full title is given below.

Many of M.B.'s books consist of a number of items. Some of these items appear in more than one of his books (or also in Herberg's volume of selections). Where this is so, and the item required may be more easily accessible in another place, alternative references (indicated by 'and') are given.

A. WORKS BY MARTIN BUBER

Ae.   'A New Venture in Adult Education'. Jerusalem:
       Hebrew University Year Book, 1950, pp. 115–23.

AJU.   *Arab–Jewish Unity*. Testimony by Judah Magnes and
       Martin Buber (for Ihud) to Anglo–American Inquiry
       Commission. London: Victor Gollancz, 1947.

As.   'Abraham the Seer'. In *Judaism* (New York), Vol. 5.
       No. 4, Fall 1956, pp. 291–305.

AT.   *At the Turning: Three Addresses on Judaism*. The Israel
       Goldstein Lectures, 1951. New York: Farrar, Straus
       and Young, 1952. Included in *Addresses on Judaism*.
       Translated by Eva Jospe. Pending from Schocken.

BMM.   *Between Man and Man*. Translated by Ronald Gregor
       Smith. London: Kegan Paul, 1947. Boston: Beacon
       Press, 1955.* London: Collins, Fontana Library, 1961.
       Translated by Ronald Gregor Smith and Maurice
       Friedman, with Introduction by Friedman. New York:
       Macmillan, 1965, with an Afterword by Martin Buber
       on 'The History of the Dialogical Principle'.

D.   *Daniel: Dialogues on Realization*. Translated with
       Introduction by Maurice S. Friedman. New York etc.:
       Holt, Rinehart and Winston, 1964.

EG.   *Eclipse of God: Studies in the Relation Between Religion and
       Philosophy*. Translated by Maurice S. Friedman, and
       others. New York: Harper and Bros. 1952. London:
       Victor Gollancz, 1953. * Harper Torchbook, 1957.

FSH.   *For the Sake of Heaven (Gog and Magog)*. Translated by
       Ludwig Lewisohn. Philadelphia: Jewish Publications
       Society, 1945. 2nd ed. with new foreword, New York:
       Harper and Bros, 1953. * New York: Meridan Books,
       1958. Harper Torchbook, 1966. Since Buber's death,
       this book has been dramatized as *The Seer* by 'Aha-
       suerus'.

GE.   *Good and Evil*. (Contains RW. and IGE. and brief
       Foreword by M.B.) New York: Charles Scribner's
       Sons, 1953.

H.   *Hasidism*. New York: The Philosophical Library, 1948.

HMM.   *Hasidism and Modern Man*. Translated and edited by

Maurice S. Friedman. New York: Horizon Press, 1958. Harper Torchbook, 1966.

IGE. *Images of Good and Evil.* Translated by Michael Bullock. (See also GE.) London: Routledge and Kegan Paul, 1952.

Ih. 'Interpreting Hasidism' in *Commentary* (New York), Vol. 36. No. 3, Sept. 1963, pp. 218–25.

IP. *Israel and Palestine: The History of an Idea.* Translated by Stanley Godman. *London: East and West Library. New York: Farrar, Straus and Young. Both 1952.

IT. *I and Thou.* Translated by Ronald Gregor Smith. Edinburgh: T. and T. Clark, 1937. 2nd (revised) edition (with a Postscript by the Author added): U.S.A. Charles Scribner's Sons, 1958. * British: T. and T. Clark, 1959.

IW. *Israel and the World: Essays in a Time of Crisis.* Translated by Olga Marx and others. New York: Schocken Books, 1948.
*2nd edition, to which two new lectures have been added, 1963.

JM. *Jewish Mysticism: and the Legends of the Baalshem.* (See also LBS.) Translated by Lucy Cohen. London and Toronto: J. M. Dent & Sons, 1931.

KG. *Kingship of God,* 3rd (enlarged) edition, translated by Richard Scheimann. London: Allen & Unwin, 1967.

KM. *The Knowledge of Man.* Translated by Maurice Friedman and Ronald Gregor Smith, with introductory essay by Friedman. * London: Allen and Unwin, 1965. New York: Harper and Row.

LBS. *The Legend of the Baal-Shem.* Translated by Maurice S. Friedman. New York: Harper and Bros, 1955. * London: East and West Library, 1956.

Lg. Letter to Gandhi, in *Two Letters to Gandhi.* Jerusalem: Rubin Mass, April 1939. (Pamphlets of *The Bond.*) Excerpts in IW., PW. and WMB.

M. *Moses.* Oxford: East and West Library, 1946.

MER. *Mamre: Essays in Religion.* Translated by Greta Hort. Melbourne University Press and Oxford University Press, 1946.

Mj.   'Myth in Judaism' (1913), the fourth of seven speeches
        on Judaism, published together in 1923, in German:
        Reden uber das Judentum. This speech only, translated by
        Ralph Manheim, in *Commentary* (New York), Vol. 9.
        No. 6, June 1950, pp. 562–6. All seven speeches to
        be included in *Addresses on Judaism*, see under AT
        above.

OMH.   *The Origin and Meaning of Hasidism*. Translated and
        edited by Maurice S. Friedman. New York: Horizon
        Press, 1960. Harper Torchbook, 1966.

PF.   *The Prophetic Faith*. Translated by Carlyle Witton-
        Davies. New York: The Macmillan Co., 1949. * Harper
        Torchbooks, 1960.

PU.   *Paths in Utopia*. Translated by R. F. C. Hull. London:
        Routledge and Kegan Paul, 1949. New York: Mac-
        millan Co., 1950. * Boston: Beacon Press, 1958.

PW.   *Pointing the Way: Collected Essays*. Translated and edited
        by Maurice S. Friedman. New York: Harper and Bros,
        1956. * London: Routledge and Kegan Paul, 1957.
        Harper Torchbook, 1963.

Rl.   'Revelation and Law.' Descriptive title of correspond-
        ence, 1922–1925, with Franz Rosenzweig. Appendix
        to N. N. Glatzer ed., *On Jewish Learning*, pp. 109–18.
        New York: Schocken Books, 1955.

RW.   *Right and Wrong, an Interpretation of some Psalms*. (See
        GE.) Translated by Ronald Gregor Smith. London:
        S.C.M. Press, 1952.

TH1.   *Tales of the Hasidim: The Early Masters*. Translated by
        Olga Marx. New York: Schocken Books, 1947. Also
        paperback, SB1. * London: Thames and Hudson,
        1956.

TH2.   *Tales of the Hasidim: The Later Masters*. Translated by
        Olga Marx. New York: Schocken Books, 1948.
        * Paperback, SB2. 1962.

TR   *Ten Rungs: Hasidic Sayings* Translated by Olga Marx.
        New York: Schocken Books, 1947. * Paperback SB.18.
        1962.

TRN.   *The Tales of Rabbi Nachman*. Translated by Maurice S.
        Friedman. New York: Horizon Press, 1956. * Paper-
        back: Indiana University Press (MB.33), 1962.

TTF. *Two Types of Faith*. Translated by Norman P. Gold-hawk. London: Routledge and Kegan Paul, 1951. New York: Macmillan Co., 1952. * Paperback: New York: Harper Torchbooks, 1961.

WM. *The Way of Man According to the Teaching of Hasidism.* * London: Routledge and Kegan Paul, 1950. Chicago: Wilcox and Follett, 1951. London: Vincent Stuart and John Watkins, 1964. (Included in HMM.)

WMB. *The Writings of Martin Buber.* Selected, edited and introduced by Will Herberg. Cleveland and New York: Meridian Books, 1956, etc. (Does not include writings on Hasidism.)

———— *The Way of Response: Martin Buber.* Selections from his Writings edited by N. N. Glatzer. New York: Schocken Books, 1966. (This more recent anthology of shorter passages includes Hasidism but does not quote from Buber's volumes of direct Biblical interpretation.)

B. WORKS ON MARTIN BUBER

The fullest assessment of Martin Buber's work is to be found in *The Philosophy of Martin Buber*, edited by Paul Arthur Schilpp and Maurice Friedman. La Salle, Illinois: The Open Court Publishing Co., London: Cambridge University Press, 1967.

Balthasar *Martin Buber and Christianity: A Dialogue between Israel and the Church*, by Hans Urs von Balthasar. Translated by Alexander Dru. London: Harvill Press, 1961.

Bgj. 'Martin Buber and German Jewry' by Ernst Simon, in *Leo Baeck Institute Year Book*, 1958. London: East and West Library.

Cohen *Martin Buber*, by Arthur A. Cohen. Studies in Modern European Literature and Thought. London: Bowes and Bowes, 1957.

Diamond *Martin Buber: Jewish Existentialist*, by Malcolm L. Diamond. New York: Oxford University Press, 1960.

Friedman *Martin Buber: The Life of Dialogue*, by Maurice S. Friedman. Chicago: University Press, 1955. * London: Routledge and Kegan Paul, 1955. * Paperback

(2nd edition, with changes, additions and supplement to bibliography), Harper Torchbooks, 1960.

Pending: *Encounter on the Ridge*, by Maurice S. Friedman, McGraw Hill. Described by publishers as 'interpretative biography, but understood not be a full biography in the accepted sense.

Kohn   *Martin Buber: Sein Werk und seine Zeit.* Ein Beitrag zur Geistesgeschichte Mitteleuropas 1880–1930. Nachwort 1930–1960 von Robert Weltsch. Joseph Melzer Verlag in Köln. 1961 edition.

Schoeps   *The Jewish–Christian Argument: A History of Theologies in Conflict*, by Hans Joachim Schoeps. Translated by David E. Green. London: Faber and Faber, 1965. (Chapter 7 quotes and discusses M.B.'s disputation with Karl Ludwig Schmidt.)

Smith   *Martin Buber*, by R. G. Smith. Makers of Contemporary Theology series. Carey Kingsgate Press. 1966. This short introductory booklet by the English translator of *I and Thou*, Professor Ronald Gregor Smith, written from a Christian standpoint, states that 'most of the theologians who have made explicit use of Buber's ideas . . . have diverted them from their original intention. And in many instances they have used them to elaborate positions which Buber himself could not accept.'

Sr.   'Jewish Adult Education in Nazi Germany as Spiritual Resistance', by Ernst Simon. In the first *Leo Baeck Institute Year Book, 1956*. London: East and West Library. (Deals largely with M.B.'s initiative and leadership.)

For a fuller list of Works on Buber, see bibliography (pp. 289–296) in 2nd edition of Friedman (above). Early in 1967, Friedman added in correspondence: 'Several new Buber books have come to my attention—an excellent dissertation on the Theological Imagination in Buber by Chris Downing, a professor of religion (in U.S.A.); two records of conversations with Buber in German by Schalom Ben-Chorin (Munich: Paul List Verlag) and Werner Kraft; and a most impressive and scholarly comprehensive treatment by Grete Schaeder in German—Martin Buber: Hebrew Humanism.'

C. OTHER WORKS QUOTED IN BRIEF

Gordis   *The Root and the Branch*, by Rabbi Robert Gordis. Chicago: University Press, 1962.

Jacobs   *Jewish Prayer*, by Rabbi Dr. Louis Jacobs. London: Jewish Chronicle Publications, 2nd edition, 1956.
Tract on Ecstasy. Translated with Introduction by Louis Jacobs. London: Vallentine, Mitchell, 1963.
Seeker of Unity, do. 1966 should be read with the *Tract*.
Principles of the Jewish Faith: An Analytical Study, do. 1964.

Schwarz-Bart   *The Last of the Just*, by André Schwarz-Bart. Translated by Stephen Becker. London: Secker and Warburg, 1961.

Scholem   *Major Trends in Jewish Mysticism*, by Gershom G. Scholem. London: Thames and Hudson, 1955.
On the Kabbalah and its Symbolism, by Gershom G. Scholem. London: Routledge & Kegan Paul, 1965.

SJE.   *Standard Jewish Encyclopaedia*. Edited by Cecil Roth. Jerusalem–Tel Aviv: Massadah Publishing Co., 1958–9.

TLS.   *The Times Literary Supplement*, London.

READING LIST

The extensive direct quotations from the works of Martin Buber in this book are intended to encourage its reader to turn to those sources. It may therefore be helpful to give a summary of the main works in each of the three categories of subject-matter:

Biblical

    IMAGES OF GOOD AND EVIL (Genesis)
    'Abraham the Seer'
    MOSES
    KINGSHIP OF GOD (Judges)
    RIGHT AND WRONG (Psalms) (also in GOOD AND EVIL)
    THE PROPHETIC FAITH
    TWO TYPES OF FAITH (Jesus)
    ISRAEL AND PALESTINE
    ISRAEL AND THE WORLD
    AT THE TURNING

Hasidic

    THE LEGEND OF THE BAAL-SHEM
    THE TALES OF RABBI NACHMAN
    TALES OF THE HASIDIM: THE EARLY MASTERS
    TALES OF THE HASIDIM: THE LATER MASTERS
    FOR THE SAKE OF HEAVEN
    TEN RUNGS
    HASIDISM AND MODERN MAN
    THE ORIGIN AND MEANING OF HASIDISM
       (includes THE WAY OF MAN)

I-Thou

    I AND THOU
    BETWEEN MAN AND MAN
    PATHS IN UTOPIA
    ECLIPSE OF GOD
    POINTING THE WAY
    THE KNOWLEDGE OF MAN

NOTES AND REFERENCES

(For abbreviated titles see preceding list)

INTRODUCTION

1. Friedman omits the earliest Buber translation into English: *Jewish Mysticism and the Legends of the Baalshem*, being a section of his work entitled 'Die Chassidischen Bucher', translated from the German by Lucy Cohen, London and Toronto, J. M. Dent & Sons Ltd., 1931. All this material except the important item 'The New Year's Sermon' is included in the later LBS.

2. The second, revised, edition (1958) contains an important postscript by Martin Buber.

3. HMM. 42.

4. MER. Except for one short item, the material in this book has reappeared, partly in H. and partly in IW. (H. has in turn been succeeded by HMM. and OMH.)

5. Rabbi A. Schuster, Ashkenazi Chief Rabbi of Amsterdam, concluded a careful article on Buber, in the congregation's journal *Ha-kehilla*, Sept./Oct. 1963, p. 8, 'Buber . . . is indeed a talented and religious-feeling Jew, but not the ambassador of Judaism. He has not accepted the religion of Israel. Hence we reject him.' This is reminiscent of the excommunication of Spinoza.

6. BMM. 33.

7. BMM. 53.

8. *Conversations of Goethe with Eckermann*, translated by John Oxenford. Everyman's Library edition, p. 173.

9. AT. 32 and WMB. 307.

10. This mis-statement is to be corrected as soon as possible.

11. Professor Erich Weniger.

12. 'Jewish Adult Education in Nazi Germany' in *Leo Baeck Institute Year Book I* (1956), London: East and West Library. This is the main source, in English, of information about Buber's work for German Jewry, 1933–38.

13. BMM. 15.

14. IW. 173–82, from which the following quotation is also taken.

15. Psalms 130, 42, 43, 6, 12, 5, 74, 64, 59, 69, 14, 10, 73, 7, 94, 4, 80, 77, 102, 120, 124, 126, 57.

16. IW. 180.

17. Hitler's massacre of European Jews did, however, have one modern antecedent that was not lost upon the Fuhrer. An important article, 'The Unremembered Genocide' by Marjorie Housepian, in *Commentary* (U.S.A.) Vol. 42, No. 3, September 1966, pp. 55–61, gives fresh and sufficiently appalling information about the Turkish massacre of the Armenians during 1915–1916 and especially

of the terrible 'death-marches'. It concludes: 'There is evidence, at any rate, that Hitler drew this conclusion (i.e. that the world cares little for the fate of those who are politically impotent). As he announced his own plans for genocide to his Supreme Commanders on August 22, 1939, he noted confidently: "Who, after all, speaks today of the annihilation of the Armenians? . . . The world believes in success alone." '

Hitler's own 'policy' towards the Jews certainly dates back at least to the early twenties:

'From his early speech of 1922, through the Nuremberg Laws of 1935 and the pogrom of November 1938 to the destruction of the Warsaw Ghetto and the death camps of Mauthausen and Auschwitz, Hitler's purpose was plain and unwavering. He meant to carry out the "extermination" of the Jewish race in Europe, using the word 'extermination' not in a metaphorical but in a precise and literal sense as the deliberate policy of the German State—and he very largely succeeded.' Alan Bullock, *Hitler —A Study in Tyranny*, revised edition, 1962, p. 407.

18. Private communication, 3.5.65.
19. BMM. 148ff.
20. IGE. 11. and GE. 65.
21. Friedman. 242. For Scheimann's translation of *Königtum Gottes*, see under Abbreviations KG above.

22. PF. 183.
23. Diamond. 211.
24. TTF. 15.
25. THι. xii.
26. KM. 7.
27. D. 147.
28. op. cit. p. 119.
29. PW. 232–3.
30. Diamond. 145–6.
31. IW. 89–90.
32. Nowadays we are usually educated to believe that reading aloud, when alone, is childish. But this stipulation is undoubtedly related to the great Oral tradition of Judaism and is an essential means of ensuring the unified participation of the whole man in the act of reading. Much depth and feeling is to be found in Buber's own writings, read in this way.
33. IW. 93.
34. Announced for publication in 1967 by Simon & Schuster Co., New York.
35. Vol. VIII. No. 4 (July/August 1965), p. 11.
36. Weekly News Bulletin, Embassy of Israel (London), 9–15 June, 1965, p. 2.
37. Quoted from Buber's religious dialogue at Stuttgart in 1933 with the evangelical theologian Karl Ludwig Schmidt by Hans Joachim Schoeps, *The Jewish-Christian Argument*—a history of theologies in conflict—translated by David E. Green. London: Faber and Faber, 1965, p. 157.

CHAPTER 1

1. TLS. 9.9.65. p. 767.
2. TLS. 29.4.65. p. 323.
3. Eugene B. Borowitz, 'Teilhard de Chardin' in *Judaism*, Vol. 14. No. 3, Summer 1965, p. 338.
4. Louis Weiwow, 'Franz Rosenzweig: a New Study' in *Quest* (annual). London: Paul Hamlyn, 1965, p. 90.
5. Gershom Scholem, *On the Kabbalah and Its Symbolism*, London: Routledge & Kegan Paul, 1965, p. 88.
6. *Ibid.*, p. 94.
7. Yehezkel Kaufman, *The Religion of Israel* (abridged). London: Allen & Unwin, 1961, pp. 6off.
8. Quotations from the fourth (1913) of Buber's *Speeches on Judaism* (*Reden über das Judentum*, 1923), as first translated into English by Ralph Manheim and published in *Commentary* (U.S.A.), Vol. 9. No. 6, June 1950, pp. 562–6. See under Abbreviations Mj. above.
9. *Ibid.*, p. 563.
10. *Ibid.*, p. 566.
11. IGE. 67 and GE. 126.
12. IGE. 69 and GE. 128.
13. According to Rabbi Robert Gordis, *The Root and the Branch*, Univ. of Chicago, 1962, p. 9. 'In traditional Judaism, the paradise tale is of course familiar and famous, but aside from a few minor references, it has developed no theological significance whatever.'
14. IGE. 13 and GE. 67–8.
15. Jewish Publication Society of America and Cambridge Univ. Press.
16. IGE. 14 and GE. 68.
17. IGE. 15 and GE. 69.
18. IGE. 15 and GE. 69.
19. IGE. 15 and GE. 69.
20. IGE. 15 and GE. 69.
21. IGE. 14–15 and GE. 68–9.
22. IGE. 20 and GE. 74–5.
23. IGE. 21 and GE. 75.
24. IGE. 22 and GE. 76.
25. IGE. 26–7 and GE. 81.
26. IGE. 34 and GE. 89.
27. IGE. 34 and GE. 88.
28. TTF. 158.
29. IW. 73.
30. Rabbi Aha, Gen. Rabbah on 49:29, cited IW. 72.
31. Notably by Gershom G. Scholem, a leading authority on the subject and author of a standard work, *Major Trends in Jewish Mysticism* (Third, revised, edition. London: Thames & Hudson, 1955). Scholem's critique, read as the Kostoria Lecture at the Institute of Jewish Studies, University College, London, was published in a somewhat different version, 'Martin Buber's Hasidism' in *Commentary* (New York), Vol. 32. No. 4, October 1961, pp. 305–316. Similar criticisms have been made by other writers, influenced by Scholem. See the contribution by Dr. Rivka Shatz-Uffenheimer in the forthcoming volume *The Philosophy of*

Martin Buber, volume 12 in the Library of Living Philosophers, Illinois: Open Court. This volume is already issued in German.

Buber replied to Scholem in an article 'Interpreting Hasidism' in *Commentary*, Vol. 36. No. 3, Sept. 1963; there was a brief rejoinder by Scholem in Vol. 37. No. 2, Feb. 1964.

32. *Liqqutei Amarim* (*Tanya*), translated by Nissan Mindel. New York: Kehot, 1962. This is a translation of Part I (almost half the full work in five parts); Parts II and III (other translators) were issued by the same publisher in 1965.

the remainder is also in preparation, by the same publisher.

Tract on Ecstasy by Dobh Baer of Lubavitch—another important doctrinal Hasidic work—has been translated by Rabbi Dr. Louis Jacobs. London: Vallentine, Mitchell, 1963. The same publisher issued Dr. Jacobs' companion volume, *Seeker of Unity* in 1965.

33. Buber revised and consolidated his main selection of the Hasidic tales in two volumes, TH1 and TH2. Two other volumes are also of great interest: LBS. and TRN. FSH. is of major importance, but differs from the other volumes in combining many fragments of traditional

narrative into a single continuous chronicle.

34. Buber consolidated his main writing about Hasidism in two volumes: HMM. and OMH. These incorporate almost all the material in the earlier volumes: MER., H. and WM.

35. Buber has published a valuable collection, to which he has given shape as a whole: TR.

36. I.e. proved true; so the leaders of the Hasidic communities are called. Buber's note.

37. WM. 13–14 and HMM. 134–5.

38. In Genesis 2:19 we read that 'the man' named 'every living creature'. In the next verse of the English translation of the Masoretic text he is 'Adam' for the first time. In Hebrew, of course, the word for 'man' and 'Adam' is the same.

39. BMM. 59.

40. Kant, Hegel, Marx, Feuerbach, Kierkegaard, Heidegger, Scheler, etc. in BMM. Spinoza, Kant, Cohen, Jung, Sartre, Heidegger, etc. EG. Marx, etc. PU. Kafka, TTF. Bergson, Weil, AT.

41. Quoted with comment, EG. 15–16.

42. EG. 18.

43. In *Power*, Bertrand Russell contends that power is the basic concept in the social sciences.

44. Quoted with comment, AT. 41.

45. AT. 44.

46. BMM. 148.

CHAPTER 2

1. PF. 92–3.
2. IGE. 60–1 and GE. 118–19.
3. As. 294–5.
4. IGE. 60 and GE. 118.
5. *King Lear*, III. iv. 105.
6. IGE. 66 and GE. 124.
7. As. 294.
8. As. 297.
9. As. 300.
10. IGE. 12 and GE. 66.
11. Genesis 4:2.
12. *Ibid.* 6:8.
13. *Ibid.* 4:24.
14. *Ibid.* 4:25, 5:3.
15. *Ibid.* 6:13.
16. *Ibid.* 9:26.
17. *Ibid.* 9:26.
18. *Ibid.* 9:6.
19. As. 294–5.
20. H. G. Wells, *The Outline of History*, 8th revision. London: Cassell & Co., 1934, pp. 254 and 264–5.
21. *Ibid.*, p. 269.
22. *Ibid.*, p. 827.
23. *Ibid.*, p. 831.
24. WMB. 12.
25. IW. 13.
26. LBS. xii–xiii.
27. Cohen, 31.
28. THI. x.
29. Louis I. Newman ed., *The Hasidic Anthology*, Schocken Books, paperback ed. 1963, p. 163—quoting Bloch, *Priester der Liebe*, pp. 37ff.
30. As. 297–8.
31. THI. 59–60.
32. LBS. 185–94.
33. IT. 3.
34. IT. 75.
35. Separately reprinted in WMB. 306–14. See also under AT.
36. Separately reprinted in W. Herberg, ed., *Four Existentialist Philosophers*, Doubleday Anchor Books, 1958, pp. 194–203. See also under AT.
37. New York, Farrar, Straus and Young, 1952.
38. PW. 220–9, with short rejoinder to critics, pp. 230–1.
39. PW. 222.
40. PW. 220–1.
41. PW. 223–4.
42. PW. 228–9.
43. PU. 132.
44. PU. 132–3.
45. IT. 56.
46. IT. 55–6.

CHAPTER 3

1. IW. 119–21.
2. As. 292.
3. As. 292.
4. As. 293.
5. Louis Jacobs, *Principles of the Jewish Faith: An Analytical Study.* London: Vallentine Mitchell, 1964, p. 14. Rabbi Dr. Jacobs' book is a comprehensive study of traditional and modern formulations of Judaism and that of Maimonides in particular.
6. *Authorized Daily Prayer Book* of the United Hebrew Congrega-

tions of the British Empire, 27th
ed., 1961. London: Eyre &
Spottiswoode, p. 90.

7. As. 298.
8. As. 297.
9. As. 297.
10. As. 298.
11. As. 298.
12. As. 298.
13. As. 299, 300.
14. As. 298.
15. As. 302.
16. As. 301.
17. As. 305.
18. THI. 244.
19. TII2. 116.
20. By Morris Joseph, p. 184n.
London: Routledge & Kegan
Paul, 4th ed., 1958.
21. Israel Abrahams, *Jewish Life in
the Middle Ages*, Meridian Books
ed., 1958, p. 62.
22. Solomon Schecter, *Studies in
Judaism* (selection from the three

series in one volume published
by The Jewish Publication
Society and Meridian Books,
1958), p. 163.

23. LBS. xiii.
24. IGE. 10–11 and GE. 64.
25. IP. 89 and TRN. 179–80.
26. IP. 93 and TRN. 186.
27. IP. 105 and TRN. 208–9.
28. IT. 124–6.
29. IT. 7–8.
30. D. 47.
31. IP. xi–xii.
32. IP. 154–61.
33. IP. 154.
34. IP. 155.
35. IP. 160.
36. IP. 160.
37. IP. 161.
38. IP. 161.
39. As. 293.
40. THI. xi–xii.
41. THI. 1.

CHAPTER 4

1. PF. 117.
2. M. 51–2.
3. M. 126.
4. IW. 28.
5. IW. 28.
6. N. N. Glatzer, ed., *Franz
Rosenzweig on Jewish Learning*,
Schocken Books, 1955, p. 22.
7. M. 157.
8. Exodus 1:18–22.
9. 1 Samuel 20:23.
10. *Ibid.* 20:17.
11. 2 Samuel 6:14.
12. Morris Joseph, *Judaism as Creed
and Life*. London: Routledge &

Kegan Paul, 4th ed., 1958, p.
34n.
13. Solomon Schecter, *Studies in
Judaism*, selected ed. New York:
Meridian Books, pp. 174–5.
14. TH2. 135.
15. Glatzer, op. cit., p. 18.
16. *Ibid.*, p. 110.
17. *Ibid.*, p. 110.
18. *Ibid.*, p. 110.
19. *Ibid.*, p. 115.
20. IW. 83.
21. IW. 86–7.
22. IW. 88.
23. IW. (2nd ed. only), pp. 256–7.

24. PW. 139–41.
25. EG. 119–20.
26. EG. 118.

27. Exodus 20:2–3.
28. IT. 42.

CHAPTER 5

1. London: Vallentine Mitchell, 1963.
2. London: *Jewish Chronicle* Publications, 2nd ed., 1956.
3. *Ibid.*, pp. 5–6.
4. *Ibid.*, p. 5.
5. New York: Schocken Books, 2nd revised ed., 1961.
6. *Ibid.*, pp. 175–6.
7. PF. 198–9.
8. RW. 44–5 and GE. 41–2.
9. Yehezkel Kaufman, *The Religion of Israel*, one volume abridgement by Moshe Greenberg. London: Allen & Unwin, 1961, p. 311.
10. PF. 200.
11. PF. 201.
12. RW. 40 and GE. 37.
13. RW. 42 and GE. 39.
14. RW. 42 and GE. 39–40.
15. PF. 201.
16. PF. 201.
17. RW. 52 and GE. 50.
18. PF. 202.
19. THI. 216.
20. TR. 75–6.
21. TR. 8.
22. TH2. 157.
23. IP. 93.
24. RW. 45 and GE. 42–3.
25. IP. 93.
26. IP. 93.
27. LBS. 18–19.
28. IT. 82.
29. IT. 118.
30. EG. 123.
31. EG. 123.
32. EG. 126.
33. BMM. 27–8.
34. BMM. 28.
35. BMM. 29.
36. BMM. 30.
37. IW. 94.
38. IW. 101–2.

CHAPTER 6

1. IW. 127.
2. *Kingship of God*, translated by Richard Scheimann, is now published. See under KG. 'Samuel and the Development of Authority in Israel' (Hebrew *Zion*, 4th year, 1f.) is described as 'part of an as yet unpublished book' (PF. 7n, 61n.) and in M. 211 (n. 105) this is referred to as *The Anointed*. Excerpts from Maurice Friedman's translation of *Elijah: A Mystery Play* appeared in the memorial issue of *Judaism*, Vol. 14. No. 3, Summer 1965, pp. 260–6.
3. IW. 130.
4. IW. 126.
5. IW. 131.
6. PW. 177–91. Quoted from shortened text in IW. 103–12.
7. IW. 107–8.

8. IW. 109–10.
9. IW. 207.
10. IW. 36.
11. IW. 36–7.
12. EG. 73.
13. THı. 86.
14. THı. 77.
15. THı. 96–7.
16. THı. 53–4.
17. THı. 172–3.
18. PF. 198.
19. IW. 112.
20. TR. 115.
21. TRN. 146

22. TRN. 148.
23. WMB. 12.
24. IW. 199–200.
25. IW. 200.
26. IW. 186–7.
27. Cohen, 35.
28. AJU.
29. IW. 255.
30. IW. 257.
31. IW. 259–60.
32. IW. 261.
33. IW. 262.
34. IW. 263.

CHAPTER 7

1. TTF. 110–11.
2. SJE.
3. Gordis, p. 10.
4. TH2. 336.
5. Schwarz–Bart, pp. 4–5.
6. PF. 231–3.
7. TTF. 12.
8. PW. 233.
9. TTF. 107–8.
10. TTF. 108–9.
11. SJE.
12. Scholem, p. 316.

13. LBS. 82–6.
14. THı. 78.
15. TH2. 151.
16. FSH. viii–ix.
17. FSH. xii–xiii.
18. TTF. 15.
19. AT. 31–2.
20. IW. 73.
21. IW. 72–3.
22. IW. 73.
23. IW. 74.
24. IW. 75–7.